Tell It Again!

Other Gryphon House books by the authors

by Shirley Raines

Story S-t-r-e-t-c-h-e-r-s

More Story S-t-r-e-t-c-h-e-r-s

Story S-t-r-e-t-c-h-e-r-s for the Primary Grades

450 More Story S-t-r-e-t-c-h-e-r-s for the Primary Grades

Never, EVER, Serve Sugary Snacks on Rainy Days

by Rebecca Isbell

The Complete Learning Center Book

Tell It Again!

Easy-to-Tell Stories with Activities for Young Children

SHIRLEY C. RAINES

REBECCA ISBELL

Cover art and illustrations by
Joan C. Waites

gryphon house
Beltsville, Maryland

Copyright © 1999 Shirley Raines and Rebecca Isbell
Published by Gryphon House, Inc.
10726 Tucker Street, Beltsville MD 20705

World Wide Web: www.gryphonhouse.com

Library of Congress Cataloging-in-Publication Data available upon publication.

Raines, Shirley C.

    Tell it again! : easy-to-tell stories with activities for young
children / Shirley C. Raines, Rebecca Isbell.

        p.   cm.
    Includes bibliographical references and index.
    ISBN 0-87659-200-0
    1. Storytelling. 2. Children's literature—Study and teaching.
3. Early childhood education—Activity programs. I. Isbell,
Rebecca T. II. Title.
LB1042.R25 1999
372.67'7–dc21   99-13675
                                                        CIP

To

Teachers and Librarians,
Mamas and Papas,
Grandfathers and Grandmothers,
Great Aunts and Great Uncles,
And Elders far and wide.
To storytellers everywhere
Who invite children
To sit by their sides.

To Lazy Jack
And Knee-High Man,
To Johnny-Cake
And Pancakes in a Pan,
To Kings and Queens
And Princesses and Such,
To goodness over wickedness,
To truth over liars.

To storytellers everywhere
Enjoy a page or two.
Then pass it on.
As Tellers of the Story,
Enjoy the magic, the tricksters, and the dreams. . .
The lessons and the schemes.
We have but one request,

Tell it again!

And tell it to the young.

Shirley Raines

Table of Contents

Introduction

The beautiful swan was once an ugly duckling. The boy who cried wolf had no help when the real wolf came. The modest turtle won the race while the boastful rabbit bragged about his speed. Some of life's greatest lessons are remembered best through the recollection of stories heard in childhood.

Storytelling involves three essential elements: the story, the teller, and the listener. A well-selected story told by an effective storyteller captivates young listeners' attention and the three elements work in harmony. The gifts of storytelling are many, including moments filled with the wonder and excitement of stories, universal truths and morals to remember and use throughout life, and the special bond that connects the storyteller and the listener.

The Power of Storytelling

Storytelling is a powerful medium. A well-told story can inspire action, foster cultural appreciation, expand children's knowledge, or provide sheer enjoyment. Listening to stories helps children understand their world and how people relate to each other in it.

When children listen to stories, they use their imaginations. They picture "nail soup" or the "teeny tiny woman" from the teller's vivid descriptions. This creativity is dependent upon the storyteller's lively telling of the story and the listener's active interpretation of what is heard. The more delightful the story and the storyteller, the more the children get out of the whole experience.

The storytelling experience also helps young children develop an appreciation of the story form. Because children are more involved in creating the pictures of the story, they are more likely to remember the characters, the sequence, and the moral of the story. Storytelling can motivate young children to explore various types of literature and become a storyteller, story reader, and story writer.

How to Select Stories to Tell Young Listeners

We wrote this book because we found few books devoted to story-telling for young children. Storytellers often have a difficult time finding the right stories for young children. We selected the stories for this book because they are excellent tales for telling that fit the developmental needs of young children.

Excellent stories for young listeners often have one or more of the following characteristics:

◉ Easy-to-follow sequence;

◉ Repetitive words and phrases;

◉ Predictable and cumulative tales;

◉ Action-packed;

◉ Often humorous;

◉ Interesting and entertaining happenings;

◉ Exciting ending with an appropriate conclusion; and

◉ Clear message or moral.

General Storytelling Tips

The following storytelling tips apply to the telling of most stories to young children.

◉ Observe the young children during the telling. Adjust and make clarifications as needed.

◉ Encourage interaction and participation.

◉ Modify the pace and length to match the experiential and developmental level of the children in the audience.

◉ Use voice variations, facial expressions, gestures, and repetitive phrases to draw the young listener into the story.

◉ Use appropriate words and descriptions that help young children imagine the happenings in their mind's eye.

◉ Retell the same story many times, since young children are building their understanding of the story.

Storytelling to young children provides special possibilities as well as unique challenges. Young children enjoy predictability, repetition, humor, and active participation in the story presentation. When stories are too complicated or the storyteller is too dramatic, the child will "turn off" or simply move away from the experience.

Design of the Book

The 18 multicultural stories in this book are grouped by common themes: Be Yourself, Using Your Wits, Appreciating Differences, and Hearing Music Everywhere. Each section contains from three to six stories and at least one of them is a well-known tale. These familiar stories are good choices for the beginning storyteller.

Each story was written to touch the hearts of young children and engage their lively minds and undivided attention. The entertainment value, the structure, and the sequence of the tales make them easy to tell. While written to be told, all the stories are strong enough to be read to children.

The layout of each story is easy to follow. Each story begins with a short introduction followed by the complete story, and ends with a simple statement of the message or moral. Storytelling tips and questions to ask children come next. Because young children learn best by doing, we included activities that enhance and enrich the experience of the story. A unique feature of the book is a collection of story cards, one for each story in the book, beginning on page 167. The card for each story includes the characters in the order they appear and an outline of the story.

Message of the Story

The message or moral of the story is included so that the storyteller can focus on the inherent value or "truth" of a story. Often the stories contain lessons that are different depending on the age of the listener. For example, in "The Nightingale," the young listener will enjoy the action of the story, the slightly older child will think more about why the Emperor preferred the mechanical bird over the real nightingale, and the adults will recognize that this is a story of the dangers of valuing possessions too much.

Storytelling Tips

We have included storytelling tips at the end of each story. These suggestions have grown from our experience telling stories to young children. The storytelling tips will help the teller identify specific aspects of the story that can be expanded and adjusted to meet the needs of the young listeners. Of course, each storyteller will make the story his or her own by selecting or modifying the suggestions so the story will relate to the specific audience.

Questions

At the end of the story, there are several questions for the storyteller to use. It is not always necessary to ask questions after the story. Good storytellers can sense the mood of the listeners and decide whether or not to ask these thought-provoking questions. Higher-level thinking and creativity are required to answer many of the questions.

Story Activities

These activities connect to the story or to the main idea of the story. The activities are open-ended to encourage young children's creativity. Many of the activities reinforce early literacy and help the child remember the main idea of the story.

Story Cards

The story cards, found at the back of the book beginning on page 167, help the storyteller to remember the order of the main characters, the sequence of events, the recurring phrases, and even the punch line. The cards will help both beginning and experienced storytellers. Use these story cards to practice telling the story until you are more comfortable with a new story, to build a collection of stories to tell, or to review stories for retelling at another time.

The Pleasure of Storytelling

What were your favorite stories as a child? Do you recall listening to "Goldilocks and the Three Bears," or "The Gingerbread Man," or "Jack and the Beanstalk?" A friend remembered her mother telling her these three classic stories. After hearing her mother tell the stories, she was startled when she went to school and the teacher read them from a book. Assuming her mother had made them up, she was surprised that teachers and parents knew the same stories.

One way to appreciate the power of the told story is to recall enjoyable stories from your childhood. Reflect on your feelings, the strength of each character, and the ways the storyteller involved you in the story. Remember being scared for Goldilocks who was lost in the forest, relieved when she spotted a charming little cottage, and anxious for her not to be caught when the bear family returned. Feel the hard, not-so-hard, and just-right bed. Taste the hot, too-cool, and the just-right porridge.

Our own delight when remembering stories and the experiences of listening should encourage us to become storytellers. Clearly the told story has found a place in literary history. How does one begin? How does one become a storyteller? Remember the stories from your past, select an appropriate story, and tell it to a child or a small group of children. Practice the tips we mention. Keep a story card handy for a quick peek, then let yourself go and enjoy the flow of the story. Observe the positive reactions of the young listeners and you will forever be a storyteller.

Whether you are a beginning teacher or an experienced librarian, a parent with a first child or a grandparent of five, the message is the same. Stories told by you are gifts that will last a lifetime. Enjoy the storytelling experience and savor the children's request when they plead,

"Tell it again!"

Be Yourself

Teeny Tiny

THIS RETOLD VERSION OF AN ENGLISH TALE IS
ABOUT A TEENY TINY WOMAN WHO FINDS A
BONE IN A GRAVEYARD AND LATER HEARS A
VOICE TELLING HER TO "GIVE IT BACK." THE
SUSPENSE BUILDS TO A SURPRISE ENDING.

BE YOURSELF

Once upon a time, there was a teeny tiny woman who lived in a teeny tiny house. One night, the teeny tiny woman couldn't sleep so she decided to take a teeny tiny walk.

So the teeny tiny woman got up from her teeny tiny bed, pulled the teeny tiny blankets up over the teeny tiny sheets and the teeny tiny pillows. She put on her teeny tiny dress with her teeny tiny shawl. She slipped her teeny tiny feet into her teeny tiny shoes.

The teeny tiny woman walked down her teeny tiny stairs, shut her teeny tiny front door, went down her teeny tiny walk to her teeny tiny gate, and out for a teeny tiny stroll.

Pretend to walk.

While she was out for her teeny tiny stroll, she walked over to the church and walked through the graveyard. There she saw a bone sticking up out of the ground. She thought, "This will make a nice treat for my teeny tiny dog, who is asleep in his teeny tiny dog bed under his teeny tiny dog blanket."

Speak in a high-pitched voice whenever the teeny tiny woman talks.

So the teeny tiny woman, using all the strength she had, tugged and pulled the bone from the ground. She brought it home past the church, through her teeny tiny gate, up her teeny tiny walk, through her teeny tiny front door and placed it in her teeny tiny cupboard.

After her walk the teeny tiny woman felt tired and sleepy so she went up her teeny tiny stairs to her teeny tiny bedroom. She took off her teeny tiny shoes, her teeny tiny shawl, and her teeny tiny dress and put on her teeny tiny sleeping gown. She pulled down the teeny tiny blanket over the teeny tiny sheets and teeny tiny pillows.

Pretend to walk up stairs.

Pretend to be asleep.

She laid her teeny tiny head upon the teeny tiny pillow and went to sleep.

As she was drifting off to sleep, she heard a voice, a tiny voice in the distance, saying, "Give me my bone!"

Pretend to pull the covers up to your chin.

The teeny tiny woman pulled the teeny tiny covers up to her chin and lay very still. Soon she heard her teeny tiny front door creak open, and the voice, closer and louder, say, "Give me my bone!"

So the teeny tiny woman slid further under the teeny tiny covers of her teeny tiny bed and tried to sleep. Then she heard a creak of her teeny tiny stairs and she heard the voice say for the third time, "Give me my bone!"

The teeny tiny woman was more than a teeny tiny bit frightened, but she tossed the teeny tiny covers off her teeny tiny head, sat up straight in her teeny tiny bed, and said in a voice that was not so teeny tiny, "TAKE IT!"

Do not take something that does not belong to you.

Storytelling Tips

◉ Speak the words that the teeny tiny woman says in a high-pitched, squeaky voice.

◉ Develop a signal for the listeners to join you in saying "teeny tiny." For example, motion with the index finger.

◉ Pantomime other actions, such as getting dressed and undressed, pulling the covers up over her head, etc.

◉ This is a spooky story that might frighten some children. When you speak the words, "Give me my bone," you can play up or tone down the scariness according to the age and reaction of your listeners. For example, use a low, growling voice to add suspense or a higher, breathier voice to create a more humorous effect.

Questions

◉ Did anything about the story make you laugh? Did anything make you feel scared?

◉ Were you surprised by the end of the story? Why?

◉ Who do you think the bone belonged to? Can you describe the person or creature?

◉ What do you think is the lesson of this story?

OLD-FASHIONED OR MODERN?

Materials

None needed

Steps

◉ Ask, is this an old-fashioned or modern story? Most children will say it is old-fashioned because the teeny tiny woman dressed in a shawl. Some versions of the story have the woman putting on her teeny tiny bonnet.

◉ Ask, what would a modern-day version of the story be like? Think of one together. Maybe the teeny tiny woman couldn't sleep, so she turned off her teeny tiny electric blanket, put on her teeny tiny jogging suit, slipped on her teeny tiny tennis shoes, put the teeny tiny lock on her door, and took her teeny tiny bicycle out for a spin around the neighborhood.

TEENY TINY MOVES

Materials

None needed

Steps

@ Invite the children to pantomime being a teeny tiny woman by taking teeny tiny steps, walking down teeny tiny stairs, getting out of a teeny tiny bed, etc.

@ Encourage the children to create a sound for the creak "c-r-e-e-a-a-k" of the front door and steps in the teeny tiny woman's house.

@ Retell the story with the listeners adding their sound effects and joining you in doing all the motions.

The
Knee-High Man

IN THIS RETOLD VERSION OF AN
AFRICAN-AMERICAN TALE, A LITTLE
MAN DECIDES HE WANTS TO BE
BIGGER AND SEEKS ADVICE FROM
THREE ANIMAL FRIENDS BEFORE
DECIDING HE IS OKAY AS HE IS.

The Knee-High Man

was just about this tall, no taller than your knees. That is why folks called him the Knee-High Man. One day the Knee-High Man was looking at himself in the mirror when he decided he wanted to get bigger, taller, and stronger. He wanted to be a sizable man.

Stand straight and tall.

So, Knee-High Man set out walking. He walked down the road until he saw a horse, a big, tall, strong horse, galloping in the pasture. He crawled through the fence, walked across the pasture, and approached the horse. He said, "Mr. Horse, you are so big, tall, and strong. Will you please tell me how I can get big, tall, and strong, like you are?"

Neigh like a horse.

"Well, you are a might short, no bigger than knee-high. All you need to do is eat lots of corn, bushels and bushels of corn, and run, and run, and run around all day."

So that is what Knee-High Man did. He ate corn until his stomach ached, then he ran and ran until his legs ached, but he didn't get any bigger or taller or stronger. He just got a stomach ache and a leg ache. He decided that Mr. Horse was wrong.

Run in place.

Knee-High man set out walking another day and he spotted a bull grazing in the pasture. He crawled through the fence, walked over, and approached the bull. He said, "Oh, Mr. Bull, you are so big, tall, and strong. Will you please tell me how I can get big, tall, and strong, like you are?"

Bellow like a bull.

"Well, you are a might short, no bigger than knee-high. All you need to do is eat lots of grass, acres and acres of grass, and bellow, and bellow, and bellow all day to get big, tall, and strong like me."

So that is what Knee-High Man did. He ate grass until his stomach ached, then he bellowed and bellowed and bellowed until his throat ached, but he didn't get any bigger or taller or stronger. He just got a stomach ache and a throat ache. He decided that Mr. Bull was wrong.

Then one day, Knee-High Man walked down the road. He walked and walked looking for someone else to ask what he should do to get bigger, taller, and stronger. He did not see anyone to ask and it was getting dark. Then he saw Mr. Hoot Owl.

Hoot like an owl.

When Knee-High Man heard Mr. Hoot Owl hooting, he thought, I always heard that Mr. Hoot Owl is wise. I will ask him.

"Mr. Hoot Owl, how can I get big and strong and tall like Mr. Horse and Mr. Bull?"

"Knee-High Man, why do you want to be big and strong and tall like Mr. Horse and Mr. Bull?"

"I want to be big and strong so that if I get in a fight no one can beat me up," said Knee-High Man.

"Has anyone ever tried to pick a fight with you?" asked Mr. Hoot Owl.

"Well, no, come to think of it, no one ever has tried to pick a fight with me," Knee-High Man remembered. "But, I want to be tall so that I can see farther."

"Climb this tree and come up here with me," said Mr. Hoot Owl, "and then you can see farther than the tallest man."

"Well, I never thought about that," said Knee-High Man.

"Hoot, hoot, well, that is what the problem is, Knee-High Man, you just don't think. You don't need to be bigger, stronger, and taller, you just need to use your brain."

Be yourself; do not envy those who are bigger, stronger, and taller than you.

Storytelling Tips

🌀 Use your hands to indicate that Knee-High Man was no taller than your knee.

🌀 Use your voice and emphasize "big" by saying, "B-i-i-i-g, like you are."

🌀 Add to Mr. Hoot Owl's personality by "hooting" each time before he speaks.

Questions

🌀 Have you ever tried anything special to make yourself stronger or taller or faster? What did you do?

🌀 Why do you want to be stronger, taller, or faster?

🌀 Is the owl always wise in the stories you hear? What other stories have a wise old owl?

IF I WERE SHORT, I COULD…

Materials

Yardstick

Steps

◉ Stand up and measure how tall you would be if you were only as high as your knee.

◉ Invite the children to imagine some of the advantages of being small. Tell them to think of all the things that they could do if they were only as tall as your knee. Some might include walking under chairs and tables, fitting into suitcases, and sleeping in drawers for beds.

◉ Pass the yardstick around and let the children measure the distance from the floor to their knees.

I NEED, I WANT

Materials

Paper and crayons

Steps

◉ Talk about the difference between needing something and wanting something.

◉ Encourage the children to remember a favorite holiday or birthday and think about the gifts that they received. Were these things that they needed or wanted?

◉ Have the children make a list or draw pictures of things they *want* and things they *need*.

The Story of the Ugly Duckling

THIS VERSION OF A HANS CHRISTIAN ANDERSEN STORY IS ABOUT AN UGLY DUCKLING WHO, AFTER BEING RIDICULED AND REJECTED, GROWS INTO A BEAUTIFUL SWAN ADMIRED BY ALL.

It was a beautiful time in the country. The pastures were green with tall grass. All around the pasture was a great forest filled with tall stately trees. Deep in the forest was a dark green lake. In a very quiet place, deep in these woods, was a mother duck sitting on her nest of eggs. She had been sitting on the nest for a long, long time. She was getting very tired and hoped the eggs would soon hatch.

After weeks of waiting, one egg began to crack. "Cheep, cheep," said the chick as she poked her head out of the egg. Then another egg cracked, then another, and then another. The chicks pecked their way out and began to cheep. The chicks began looking around the nest and saying, "What a big world this is!"

Smile and look proud.

The mother duck was very pleased with the lovely ducklings she had hatched. She started to get up from the nest to show them their big beautiful world. Just as she was getting up from her nest, she noticed that the biggest egg in her nest had not hatched. She wondered, "How much longer is this big egg going to take?" So she sat back on the egg and continued to keep it warm so it would hatch, too.

Finally, after several more weeks, the big egg began to crack. "Cheep, cheep" said the last chick. He pulled and pecked himself out of the shell.

Look confused.

The mother duck looked at the chick and said, "How big and ugly he is. He doesn't look like any of my other ducklings."

The next day the mother duck took her family down to the lake. She splashed in the cool clear water in the lake and called to the ducklings to join her, "Quack, quack." One by one the ducklings splashed into the lake, went under the water, and came floating to the top. Their feet paddled as they swam around the lake in a line right behind their mother. The big gray duckling followed along at the very end of the line.

Quack in an encouraging voice.

The mother and the ducklings swam down to the duck yard where the other ducks lived. When the other ducks saw the new mother and the ducklings, they all said, "What a fine family you have and the ducklings are so beautiful. All except the big one, who is very ugly." The other ducks began to quack very loudly. "How ugly that big duckling is! We can't stand him." The big ducks begin to fly at him and peck him on the neck and the head.

Quack and speak in a loud mean voice.

"Leave him alone, he is not hurting anyone," said the mother duck. But the ducks would not listen and continued to peck the big ugly duckling. They called him names and told him how ugly he was.

Each day things got worse for the big duckling. He was chased by the ducks, pecked by the hens, and even the little girl who brought food pushed him away. Finally it became too much for him. He could not stand the harsh words from the ducks. Even his brothers and sisters told him he was ugly. He ran off to hide in the hedge at the edge of the pond where no one could see how ugly he was. In the marsh he found some wild ducks. They inquired, "What kind of creature are you? You are terribly ugly." After a few days, he decided to move on to another place.

Pretend to be the ugly duckling looking sad.

Shake your head and look surprised.

At the edge of the woods the ugly duckling found an old cottage. An old woman lived there with a cat that could arch his back and a hen that could lay eggs. When the old woman saw the big duckling, she said, "What on earth are you? You are so big and ugly!" She decided to let the ugly duckling stay for three weeks to see if it would lay eggs. The big duckling sat in the corner of the dark cold house and thought about the fresh air and sunshine at the lake. The gloomy place was too sad so the duckling left the cottage and went back to the lake.

It was winter on the lake and the water had become very cold. The ugly duckling floated on the water and ducked his head in the cool mist. The sky became dark and the wind blew cold. Snow and hail began to fall and covered the duckling swimming in the lake. The ugly duckling swam in circles to keep the water from freezing around him. He became so tired that he couldn't swim anymore.

Move in circles, then sit down as if unable to move.

Soon he was frozen in the water, unable to move. A farmer saw the ugly ducking frozen in the pond. He chipped the ice away and took the ugly duckling home with him to nurse him back to health. When his wife saw the duckling, she screamed and threw a pot at him because he was so big and ugly. The children chased him and told him how ugly he was. Luckily the back door was open so the duckling flew out into the bushes and lay there exhausted. It was a miserable winter for the duckling as he tried to survive on his own deep in the marsh.

One day the sun began to shine and it became much warmer than before. The birds began to sing. The marsh grass was turning green. A beautiful spring was coming to the lake and the marshes where the duckling had been hiding all winter. The ugly duckling felt the warm sun and he heard the birds singing. He pulled himself into the warm lake water.

A flock of beautiful white birds was flying in the sky above the marsh. They were dazzling—with long necks and broad, powerful wings. They gracefully circled the lake and majestically landed on the still lake water. The duckling watched the beautiful birds and admired their long necks and snowy white feathers. The ducking wanted to swim to the beautiful birds but he was afraid. "I am so ugly they will not want me close to them, they will peck me and call me ugly names." But somehow he seemed to be drawn to them, so he swam in their direction.

Stretch your neck out and stroke your "feathers."

As he swam he looked into the water below him and saw his reflection. He saw himself in the clear water. He was not an ugly dark gray duckling anymore; he had become a beautiful white swan. The big beautiful swans swam in circles around him. They stroked his neck with their bills. They were very happy to see him. Some children in the park saw the swans. They cried, "A new swan has come." They threw him bread and said, "The new swan is the prettiest, he is so strong and handsome."

The swan shook his feathers and raised his slender neck and said, "I never dreamed of such happiness, when I was the ugly duckling."

Do not make fun of others.

THE STORY OF THE UGLY DUCKLING

StorytellingTips

◉ Be sensitive to the feelings and ages of the young children in the audience. It is essential that the children understand that the characters in the story thought the young duckling was ugly because it looked different from the other ducks. Be careful not to humiliate and ridicule the duckling too much. Observe the children's responses and adjust the content so the feelings aroused are not too intense.

◉ Develop a distinct way of saying "ugly" so that it sounds "ugly." Use this same inflection each time the word is said by the mother duck, other ducks, and people. The word "beautiful" is also used many times in the last segments of the story. Use a lyrical inflection as you repeat this word in the telling. Remember that young children will use these words in their conversations and play after they have heard the story, demonstrating their expanding vocabulary.

◉ This story is long and includes many different settings. It works best with listeners who have heard a number of other told stories. Because each segment is so important to the story, it is not a good idea to shorten the content but rather to wait until the listeners are ready to hear a long story.

Questions

◉ How do you think the ugly duckling felt when all the ducks were making fun of him?

◉ What did the swans look like? How did the ugly duckling know that he was a swan, too?

◉ How do you think the ugly duckling felt about other "ugly ducklings" that he saw? How do you think he treated them?

MIX AND MATCH

Materials

A picture book that includes baby and adult animals. Try to find one that includes swans and ducks.

Steps

◉ Read the book and talk about the pictures in the book.

◉ Point out the ways a baby animal and an adult animal are the same and different.

◉ A trip to the zoo or duck pond would be a fun follow-up to this story.

GROWING EVERY DAY

Materials

A collection of
baby pictures
and current
photographs

Steps

◉ Look at the
pictures of
babies. Talk
about what
babies look
like and
what they
can do.

◉ Examine pictures of older children. What can older children do?

◉ Sort the pictures into categories of baby or child. Discuss how the
two are similar and how they are different.

Using Your Wits

Three Billy Goats Gruff

THIS RETOLD VERSION OF THE
NORWEGIAN FOLKTALE IS ABOUT HOW A
LITTLE BILLY GOAT OUTWITS A MEAN
TROLL WHO LIVES UNDER A BRIDGE.

Once upon a time there were three billy goats whose family name was Gruff. The three brothers were Little Billy Goat Gruff, Middle-Sized Billy Goat Gruff, and Great Big Billy Goat Gruff. They grazed on the lush green grass that grew on the hillsides. Middle-Sized Billy Goat and Great Big Billy Goat often warned Little Billy Goat not to wander far from home.

"Don't go across the bridge. There is a mean old troll who lives under the bridge. He eats little billy goats. Always stay on this side of the bridge."

Little Billy Goat, being an obedient little brother, always listened to the advice of Middle-Sized Billy Goat and Great Big Billy Goat Gruff. But one day, he grazed all the green grass on the little hillside near their home. He nibbled the grass right up to the edge of the wooden bridge.

When he looked across the bridge, there on the other side was a grassy hillside, with green, green grass. He thought to himself, "If I could just graze on that green, green grass, I could grow big and strong like my middle-sized brother, maybe even as big and strong as my great big brother." He looked longingly across to the hillside and glanced down under the bridge. He didn't see the troll, so he decided to cross the bridge. Trip-trap, trip-trap, trip-trap, Little Billy Goat Gruff came trip-trapping across the wooden bridge. Suddenly he heard the troll say, "Who is that trip-trapping across my bridge?"

Use a high voice every time the Little Billy Goat speaks.

"It is Little Billy Goat Gruff."

The troll replied, "Little Billy Goat Gruff, I love to eat little billy goats and I am going to eat you up!"

Use a strong voice every time the troll speaks.

Little Billy Goat Gruff, being a smart little goat, answered, "Oh, Mr. Troll, you don't want to eat me. I am just a little billy goat. Wait for my brother who is much bigger than I am, then you would have more to eat."

The troll, thinking how nice it would be to have a big meal of billy goat, replied, "But, how do you know your brother will come to my bridge?"

"Mr. Troll, when my brother cannot find me he will come looking for me. When he sees me eating the green, green grass across this bridge, he will come to fetch me home." And so, Mr. Troll waited while Little Billy Goat Gruff trip-trapped, trip-trapped, trip-trapped across the wooden bridge and up the hill to the green, green grass on the other side.

Put you hand across your forehead to look in the distance.

Soon, Middle-Sized Billy Goat Gruff spotted his brother eating the green, green grass across the bridge. He decided to go get his little brother to bring him home. Trip-trap, trip-trap, trip-trap, Middle-Sized Billy Goat Gruff came trip-trapping across the wooden bridge. Suddenly, he heard the mean old troll say, "Who is that trip-trapping across my bridge?"

"It is Middle-Sized Billy Goat Gruff."

Speak in a deep and loud voice every time Middle-Sized Billy Goat speaks.

The troll growled, "Middle-Sized Billy Goat Gruff, I love to eat middle-sized goats and I am going to eat you up!"

Middle-Sized Billy Goat Gruff, being a smart middle-sized goat, answered, "Oh, Mr. Troll, you don't want to eat me. I am just a middle-sized billy goat. Wait for my brother who is much bigger than I am, then you would have more to eat."

The troll, thinking how nice it would be to have a great big meal of billy goat, said, "But, how do you know your brother will come to my bridge?"

"Mr. Troll, when my brother cannot find me he will come looking for me. When he sees me eating the green, green grass on the hillside across this bridge, he will come to fetch me home."

And so, Mr. Troll waited while Middle-Sized Billy Goat Gruff trip-trapped, trip-trapped, trip-trapped across the wooden bridge and up the hill to join his little brother and eat the green, green grass on the other side.

Soon, Great Big Billy Goat Gruff, spotting his two brothers grazing on the green, green grass across the bridge, decided to go get his brothers to bring them home. Trip-trap, trip-trap, trip-trap, Great Big Billy Goat Gruff came trip-trapping across the wooden bridge. As expected, the troll growled, "Who is that trip-trapping across my bridge?"

Speak in a very loud and very deep voice every time the Great Big Billy Goat speaks.

"It is Great Big Billy Goat Gruff."

The troll growled, "Great Big Billy Goat Gruff, I love to eat great big billy goats and I am going to eat you up!"

Great Big Billy Goat Gruff, being a quick-thinking great big billy goat, answered, "Oh, Mr. Troll, I don't think you are going to eat me. Just come up and see how big I am and how tough I would be to eat."

Look far, far away.

The mean old troll crept up the banks of the creek and over the edge of the bridge. Great Big Billy Goat Gruff stood in the middle of the wooden bridge and lowered his head. He butted that mean old troll off the bridge, up into the air, and far, far down the river. When the troll landed, he ran off to another bridge and another hillside.

Now, every day, the three Billy Goats Gruff cross the wooden bridge to graze on the green, green grass on the hillside. I can just hear them now crossing the bridge.

Trip-trap, trip-trap, trip-trap. Trip-trap, trip-trap, trip-trap. Trip-trap, trip-trap, trip-trap.

Don't let others bully you.

Storytelling Tips

⦿ Speak in a high voice for the Little Billy Goat Gruff, a deeper and louder voice for the Middle-Sized Billy Goat Gruff, and a very deep and very loud voice for the Great Big Billy Goat Gruff.

⦿ Each time the troll speaks, use distinctive hand gestures and facial expressions.

⦿ Encourage the listeners to say the trip-trap, trip-trapping sounds as you tell the story.

⦿ Experiment with different sound effects for the trip-trapping of the three billy goats. You might tap the ends of your fingers together for the Little Billy Goat Gruff, pat your knees for the trip-trapping of the Middle-Sized Billy Goat Gruff, and slap your thighs for the Great Big Billy Goat Gruff.

⦿ Invite the listeners to rap their knuckles on something wooden to make the sound of trip-trapping on the wooden bridge.

Questions

⦿ What experiences have you had with a bully? What happened?

⦿ Do you think the phrase, "The grass is always greener on the other side," applies in this story? What do you think the phrase means?

⦿ Can you think of any other way the billy goats might have outwitted the troll?

MOLD IT!

Josh

Materials

Playdough • plastic knives • large index cards • marker

Steps

◉ Talk about the troll and how silly he might look.

◉ Invite the children to each sculpt one character from the story.

◉ Demonstrate how to use the plastic knife to cut features into the playdough.

◉ Fold the index cards in half. Print "sculpted by" and each child's name on a card.

◉ Display the playdough sculptures of the billy goats and the troll in a prominent place for everyone to admire.

TRIP-TRAPPING

Materials

Sturdy, low wooden table

Steps

◉ The listeners decide which roles they want to assume.

◉ Provide a sturdy, low wooden table to use as the bridge.

◉ Decide how to make the trip-trapping sounds. Try rapping knuckles on the wooden table; saying the words outloud; or patting fingertips, knees, or thighs.

◉ The storyteller could sit under the table, telling the story and pretending to be the mean old troll.

◉ Take turns being the different billy goats (the youngest or smallest child does not always have to be the little billy goat).

HUNT FOR THREES

Materials

Sets of three ordinary household objects that come in different sizes, such as cups, plates, bowls, pieces of paper, crayons, pencils, toy cars, books, dolls, stuffed animals • large table

Steps

◉ Talk about the sizes of the three billy goats in the story.

◉ Mix up all the objects and place them on a large table.

◉ Encourage the listeners to select an object, find it in all three sizes, and then order the objects by size.

◉ Make it more challenging by grouping two objects together and then make three sets with the groups. For example, the set might be a little sheet of paper and a short pencil; followed by a middle-sized sheet of paper and a middle-length pencil; followed by a great big sheet of paper and a full-length pencil.

The Turtle and the Rabbit

IN THIS ADAPTATION OF THE CLASSIC
AESOP FABLE, A VERY FAST RABBIT
CHALLENGES A SLOW TURTLE TO A RACE
BUT LOSES WHEN HE STOPS
TO TAKE A NAP.

Once there was a rabbit who was very proud. He considered himself to be the finest rabbit in all the land. The rabbit was proud of how fast he could run. He had very strong back legs that helped him run like the wind. He never missed the opportunity to show off his running skills to his friends and to remind them how fast he could run.

Pretend to run.

One day he was bragging to his friends and showing them how very fast he could run. As he was running, he jumped over a shell in the road. Slowly a head and legs came out of the shell and it began to move along the road. The rabbit realized that it was a turtle, slowly crawling down the road.

"What a slow creature you are," said the rabbit to the turtle. "You are so slow. I don't know why you bother to move at all." The rabbit laughed at the joke he had made about the turtle.

The turtle looked at the rabbit coolly and said, "Each animal moves at his own pace. I may creep along slowly but I get where I want to go. In fact I could get there quicker than you, fast as you are."

Hold your stomach and pretend to laugn.

The rabbit thought this was very funny. He laughed at the idea of a turtle being faster than him. "What nonsense," said the rabbit. "How could you possibly be faster than me? I can run as fast as the wind. You crawl along so slowly it is hard to tell if you are moving at all. Quicker than me? I would like to see that."

So the rabbit challenged the turtle to a race so they could see who was really the fastest. The race was set for the next day. Everyone turned out to see the race between the fast rabbit and the slow turtle.

The fox counted down for the start of the race. "Five, four, three, two, one, go." With a bound the rabbit speedily fled out of sight. The turtle slowly lifted one foot and then another as he kept his eyes on the winding road in front of him. The rabbit raced along the road. Each time he would see a crowd of people lining the **Wave.** road he would turn and wave. He wanted them to know how fast he could run. Far, far behind was the turtle slowly lifting one leg and then another, always keeping his eyes on the road in front of him.

Soon the fast rabbit came to a marker on the road. The marker showed that he had run half the distance of the race. He couldn't see the turtle at all.

The rabbit thought, "I am so far ahead and that turtle is so slow that he is miles behind me. It will be a long time **Stretch, yawn,** before that slowpoke turtle will be **then close your** here. I think I will lie down and take a **eyes.** little rest in the warm sun. There will be plenty of time to win the race when I wake up."

Meanwhile, way back down the road, the turtle continued to slowly crawl along, never stopping. He steadily **Move your** moved first with one foot and then the other, with his **arms and legs** eyes always on the road in front of him. As the day **slowly and** passed, the rabbit continued to sleep. The slow and **steadily.**

steady turtle kept moving. He didn't stop to rest. He moved slowly along the road. Eventually the slow and steady turtle passed the rabbit who was still sleeping by the side of the road. The rabbit was sleeping so soundly that he didn't hear the turtle pass him. When the rabbit finally awoke from his long nap, he looked behind him to see where the turtle was. He didn't see the turtle. He said, "That turtle is slower than I thought. It will be midnight before he gets to the finish line."

Open your mouth in mock surprise.

The rabbit stretched his legs and got back on the road to continue the race. The rabbit ran down the road and over the hill. Then he saw the most amazing sight—at the finish line was the turtle. The crowds were cheering as the turtle broke the tape at the end of the race. The turtle was declared the winner of the race. The rabbit was gasping for breath and the turtle was smiling. "How, when, where?" spluttered the rabbit.

The turtle said, "I passed you while you were sleeping. I may be slow but I kept my eye on the goal. By being slow and steady, I won the race."

Keep your eye on the goal and keep going.

Storytelling Tips

🌀 Emphasize the difference between the fast rabbit and the slow turtle by using a quick rhythmic pattern when the rabbit speaks and a slow deliberate pattern when the turtle speaks. Practice using these techniques so that they support the story rather than distract the listeners.

🌀 For young listeners, present the story with little elaboration; for older or more experienced listeners, include more details of the rabbit's experiences while running so fast.

🌀 Add sound effects such as the turtle crawling, produced by slow scraping fingers across the top of legs; the rabbit running, produced by fast hand slapping; cheering crowds, produced by hand clapping. Ask the listeners for suggestions for sound effects.

Questions

🌀 What are some of the things rabbit did that showed how proud he was of his running ability?

🌀 How did the turtle win the race?

🌀 If you were in a race, how would you want to run? Would it be more like rabbit or more like turtle?

TELL IT AGAIN

Materials

None needed

Steps

 Retell the story, either immediately after the first telling if the listeners are still interested, or on another day. Often, listeners say, "Tell it again!" at the end of a story. This retelling helps the listeners clarify their understanding of events or characters.

Review the story. Talk about what happened first and what happened next, so that the sequence of events is clear. Always talk about how the story began and ended, for these are two elements young listeners often use in retelling.

Ask the listeners to tell you the story. Accept all levels of retelling. In these beginning experiences the goal is to build confidence in storytelling abilities, not to make sure every detail is correct. Let the child know you enjoyed the special way she shared the story. Do not be concerned if a listener doesn't want to tell the story in front of a group. Suggest that she share the story with a favorite stuffed animal or friend. Sometimes a child who doesn't want to tell a story can be heard later on telling the story to her teddy bear—a safe beginning for the budding storyteller.

MOVING DOWN THE ROAD

Materials

None needed

Steps

◉ Talk about how the rabbit moves and how the turtle moves.

◉ Move like a rabbit or a turtle.

◉ Discuss how they move differently.

◉ Take turns being turtles and rabbits so everyone has an opportunity to move in both ways.

Nail Soup

THIS STORY IS BASED ON A
CZECHOSLOVAKIAN FOLKTALE
ABOUT HOW A TRAMP TRICKS A
WOMAN INTO MAKING SOUP BY
COOKING A NAIL.

Once upon a time, a tramp, with his bundle slung over his shoulder, walked along a lonely road. As night approached, the tramp saw a small cottage at the edge of the woods. The sunset reflecting on the windows of the cottage gave it a welcoming glow.

Pretend to sling a bundle over your shoulder.

So the tramp walked up to the door and knocked. An old woman answered the door. She scowled as she said, "Don't ask for any food, because I have none."

Seeing the fire burning in the fireplace, the tramp asked if he could come and sit by the fire and warm himself. The old woman replied, "Oh, all right. I guess it won't hurt anything. The fire can burn for two as easy as it can for one."

So the tramp put his bundle in the corner and sat upon the stool near the warm fire. In a few minutes, his stomach began to growl. He was very hungry. But the old woman said, "There is no food to eat."

The tramp took a nail from his pocket and held it up in the light of the fire as if to admire it. "What is that nail for?" asked the old woman.

Pretend to hold up a nail.

"Well, Madam, you may never believe it, but last night, I ate the finest soup I've ever eaten, and the main ingredient was this nail."

"Nail soup? Nail soup? That is ridiculous!" the woman scoffed, but she was curious.

"Yes, Madam, it is true. I boiled this nail in a pot of hot water. It was delicious," he assured her.

"Delicious? Delicious? How can you make delicious soup from a nail? I must see how it is done," she said, as she went off to get the pot for boiling water.

The old woman handed a big pot over to the tramp. He filled it half full of water and placed it on the stove. Then, he lifted the lid and dropped in the nail. With much ceremony, he put the lid back on the pot, then returned to sit on his stool by the fire.

Pretend to lift a pot lid and sniff the aroma.

He waited patiently. When he heard the water boiling, he lifted the lid. "Nail soup, delicious nail soup. Madam, when I cooked the soup last night, all it needed was some salt and pepper. I don't suppose you have a bit of salt and some pepper, do you? The batch of soup that I made last night just needed some salt and pepper to make it just right."

"Salt and pepper? I might just have some salt and pepper left in this empty cupboard," she said.

Pretend to shake salt and pepper shakers.

The tramp ceremoniously added the salt and pepper into the bubbling water with the nail. He put the lid back on the large soup pot and returned to sit on his stool by the fire.

The old woman, curious about the soup, lifted the lid to check inside. Just as she lifted the lid, the tramp asked, "Madam, might you have just half an onion to add to the delicious nail soup? The batch of soup that I made last night just needed half an onion to make it just right.

"Half an onion? I might just have half an onion left in this cupboard," she said. As she cracked open the door and slid out the onion, the tramp spied other vegetables upon the shelves, but he pretended not to notice. Instead he replied, "Yes, half an onion will make it just right." He slipped the onion into the pot of boiling water, with the salt and pepper, and one gleaming nail.

When the onion had been cooking in the pot and the aroma filled the little house, the old woman lifted the lid to check inside. Just as she lifted the lid, the tramp asked, "Madam, might you have just a few carrots to add to this delicious nail soup? The batch of soup that I made last night just needed a few carrots to make it just right."

Pretend to smell delicious soup.

"A few carrots? I might just have a few carrots left in this cupboard," she said. When she went to the cupboard, cracked open the door, and slid out the carrots, the tramp spied other vegetables. Again, he pretended not to notice. Instead, he replied, "Yes, a few carrots will make it just right."

He slipped the carrots into the pot of boiling water, with half of an onion, the salt and pepper, and one gleaming nail.

Encourage listeners to repeat "one gleaming nail."

The tramp returned to sit on his stool by the fire. The old woman was getting hungry now. She went to check the soup. Just as she lifted the lid, the tramp asked, "Madam, might you have just a few small potatoes to add to this delicious nail soup? The batch of soup that I made last night just needed a few potatoes to make it just right."

"A few potatoes? I might just have a few potatoes left in this cupboard," she said. She went to the cupboard, cracked open the door, gathered up the potatoes, washed them, diced them, and brought them to the tramp. He said in quite a matter-of-fact way, "Yes, a few

Pretend to dice potatoes.

potatoes will make it just right." He plopped the potatoes into the pot of boiling water, with a few carrots, half an onion, some salt and pepper, and one gleaming nail.

The tramp returned to sit on his stool by the fire. The old woman was ferociously hungry now. She went to check the soup. Just as she lifted the lid, the tramp asked, "Madam, might you have a cabbage, even just a little head, to add to this delicious nail soup? The batch of soup that I made last night just needed a small head of cabbage to make it just right."

"A small head of cabbage? I might just have a small head of cabbage left in this cupboard," she said. She went to the cupboard, cracked open the door, and lifted a small head of cabbage from its place in the corner. She brought the cabbage to the tramp. He said in quite a matter of fact way,

"Yes, a small head of cabbage will make it just right." He peeled the cabbage leaves into the pot of boiling water, with the potatoes, a few carrots, half an onion, some salt and pepper, and one gleaming nail.

Pretend to smell the delicious soup. Yum!

The tramp returned to sit on his stool by the fire. Now, the soup was bubbling and churning with good vegetables. The tramp invited the old lady to stir the soup and smell the delicious aroma. Although she agreed that it smelled delicious, she said, "A bit of meat is what we need to add to this batch of soup to make it just right."

The old woman returned with some cooked roast beef and chopped it into small pieces. "Yes," she said," a bit

USING YOUR WITS

of roast beef will make it just right." She dropped the roast beef into the pot of boiling water with the small head of cabbage, some potatoes, a few carrots, half an onion, some salt and pepper, and one gleaming nail.

Hold up one finger.

The old woman and the tramp returned to sit by the fire. Soon, the old woman asked, "Shall we eat? The soup smells ready." The tramp looked around at the lovely cloth she was stitching, the candlestick on the mantel, and two beautiful bowls that sat upon a shelf.

Pretend to look around the room.

"Madam," he said, "since you added the lovely pieces of roast beef, this delicious soup is now fit for a king and queen. Shall we set the table like royalty?"

With a smile on her face, the old woman placed the beautiful cloth on the rough kitchen table. She took the candlestick from the mantel by the fire. She brought lovely silver spoons from a drawer. She took down the beautiful bowls that sat upon the shelf and filled them with the delicious soup.

Pretend to admire the table.

The tramp looked at the table fit for a king and queen and said, "Madam, the batch of soup that I made last night would have been just right, if we had a loaf of bread to accompany our delicious nail soup."

"A loaf of bread? I might just look in the bread box to see if a crust of bread might remain." She went to the bread box and opened it. There was a lovely loaf that looked like it had been baked that very day.

The tramp clasped his hands together and declared, "Dear Madam, I shall be honored to share my delicious nail soup with you."

Yawn and close your eyes.

They sat at the lovely table, ate their delicious soup, and talked of many journeys the tramp had made all across the country. It was a delightful evening, but the old woman was warm from the soup and tired from her gardening. Reluctantly she decided it was time to go to bed, but not before she invited the tramp to sleep in front of the warm fire.

The next morning, at breakfast, they ate another bowl of soup. The old woman said, "I don't know when I ever enjoyed an evening more than last night or have eaten a better bowl of soup."

As the tramp rose to leave, the old woman said, "Thank you for showing me how to make nail soup."

"No, no, it is I who must thank you," said the tramp. "It was what you added that made the difference!"

The old woman stood at the cottage door with a smile on her face.

Pretend to pat a pocket.

And the tramp walked on down the road, whistling as he went. He paused just a minute and patted the nail in his pocket just to make sure it was still there.

Share what you have and enjoy the company of those who come your way.

Storytelling Tips

◉ Explain that the word "tramp" means a person who travels from place to place looking for work.

◉ Stretch out the repetition of the phrase "just right" to "j-u-u-u-s-t right."

◉ Encourage listeners to join in the tramp's refrain, "Yes, a _____ will make it just right."

◉ Invite the children to repeat the old woman's phrase when she answers the tramp after each of his requests (e.g., "Half an onion? I might just have half an onion...").

◉ Practice telling the story with the old woman scowling at the beginning, and the tramp acting very polite. Show the change in the old woman's disposition when she shared food and conversation with someone.

Questions

◉ Do you know a story where soup was made from a stone?

◉ What do you think the tramp will have for supper the next night?

◉ If you wanted to make delicious soup, what would you put into it?

SHOPPING FOR NAIL SOUP

Materials

Shopping list of ingredients for nail soup • notepad

Steps

◉ Invite the children to help you make a list of all the ingredients in nail soup.

◉ Go to the grocery store and buy the ingredients. Let the children help locate the items in the supermarket. Show where the price is listed.

◉ Count the number of items on the list and count the number of ingredients you bought at the store.

◉ Check off the items from the list to make certain you have everything.

◉ For older listeners, actually calculate the price of a bowl of nail soup. Don't forget the price of a nail!

RECIPE FOR NAIL SOUP

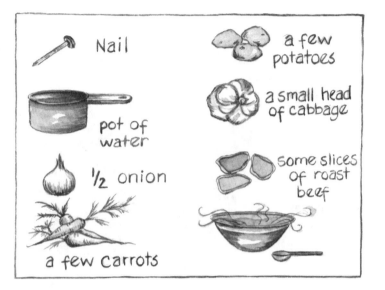

Materials

Paper marker • one very clean nail • soup pot • water • salt and pepper • half an onion • a few carrots • a few potatoes • a small head of cabbage • some slices of roast beef • a loaf of bread • a blunt knife • lovely tablecloth • candles • soup bowls • spoons

Steps

◉ Ask the children to recall the ingredients for nail soup. Print the list like a recipe.

◉ Prepare the vegetables: cut and chop the carrots and cabbage, dice the potatoes, and slice the onion.

◉ Add the vegetables to the soup in the same order as the ingredients were added in the story. Be sure to start with one gleaming nail.

◉ After the soup is cooked, set a lovely table and enjoy the soup.

◉ If you dare, serve nail soup for breakfast the next morning.

ANOTHER DAY

Materials

None needed

Steps

🌀 Ask, what did the tramp do the next night? Do you think that he made nail soup again with someone else?

🌀 Act out the story together by pretending to be the tramp and another old woman who lives in a house just down the road.

🌀 If necessary, coach the listeners through the story. If a young listener is involved, use a real pot and the real ingredients as cues to remember what comes next in the story. For older listeners, just pantomime motions.

Johnny-Cake

IN THIS RETOLD VERSION OF AN
ENGLISH FOLKTALE, A JOHNNY-CAKE
IS CHASED BY A BOY, HIS PARENTS,
SOME DIGGERS, A BEAR, AND A
WOLF, BUT IS FINALLY CAUGHT BY A
SLY FOX.

Once upon a time, there was a little old man and a little old woman who had a little boy. One day the little old woman decided to make round Johnny-Cake for lunch. The little old woman told the little boy to watch the oven so that the Johnny-Cake did not get too brown. Then, the little old woman and the little old man went out to weed the vegetable garden.

The little boy was busy playing, so he forgot to watch the oven and take out the Johnny-Cake. Suddenly he heard a bang. The oven got so hot that the oven door flew open and out rolled the Johnny-Cake. It rolled out the kitchen door and down the garden path. The little boy shouted and chased after the rolling Johnny-Cake. He yelled, "Stop, stop, stop, Johnny-Cake!" When his parents heard the yelling, they chased the Johnny-Cake, too. But they were soon out of breath and sat down on the side of the road.

Roll your hands one over the other.

Johnny-Cake rolled on until he passed two well diggers. The well diggers yelled, "Johnny-Cake, where are you going so fast?"

Roll hands again.

Johnny-Cake replied, "I ran faster than the little boy, the little old man, and the little old woman, and I can run faster than you, too-oo-o!" as he rolled on.

Pant.

The well diggers said, "Well, we are faster than they are." They started to chase Johnny-Cake, but they were soon out of breath and sat down on the side of the road.

Johnny-Cake rolled on until he passed two ditch diggers. The ditch diggers yelled, "Johnny-Cake, where are you going so fast?"

USING YOUR WITS

Johnny-Cake replied, "I ran faster than the little boy, the little old man and the little old woman, and two well diggers, and I can run faster than you, too-oo-o!" as he rolled on.

Roll hands again.

The ditch diggers said, "Well, we are faster than they are." They started to chase Johnny-Cake, but they were soon out of breath and sat down on the side of the road.

Pant.

Johnny-Cake rolled on until he passed Bear. Bear growled, "Johnny-Cake, where are you going so fast?"

Johnny-Cake replied, "I ran faster than the little boy, the little old man and the little old woman, two well diggers and two ditch diggers, and I can run faster than you, too-oo-o!" as he rolled on.

Roll hands again.

Pant.

Bear said, "Well, I am faster than they are." Bear started to chase Johnny-Cake, but he was soon out of breath and sat down on the side of the road.

Johnny-Cake rolled on until he passed Wolf. Wolf howled, "Johnny-Cake, where are you going so fast?"

Johnny-Cake replied, "I ran faster than the little boy, the little old man and the little old woman, two well diggers, two ditch diggers, and Bear, and I can run faster than you, too-oo-o!" as he rolled on.

Roll hands again.

Wolf said, "Well, I am faster than they are." Wolf started to chase Johnny-Cake, but he was soon out of breath and sat down on the side of the road.

Pant.

Roll hands again.

Johnny-Cake rolled on until he passed Fox. Fox grinned and said, "Johnny-Cake, where are you going so fast?"

Johnny-Cake replied, "I ran faster than the little boy, the

little old man and the little old woman, two well diggers, two ditch diggers, Bear, and Wolf, and I can run faster than you, too-oo-o!" as he rolled on.

Fox said, "What did you say? Come closer, I can't hear you." Fox turned his head as if to listen better.

Roll hands again.

Johnny-Cake moved closer and replied, "I ran faster than the little boy, the little old man and the little old woman, two well diggers, two ditch diggers, Bear, and Wolf, and I can run faster than you, too-oo-o!" as he rolled on.

But Fox said, "Come closer, Johnny-Cake, I can't hear you, you are too far away." Fox leaned forward turning his head as if to hear what Johnny-Cake had to say.

Roll hands again.

Johnny-Cake moved even closer and replied, "I ran faster than the little boy, the little old man and the little old woman, two well diggers, two ditch diggers, Bear, and Wolf, and I can run faster than you, too-oo-o!" as he rolled on.

Fox said, "You can, can you?" and quickly opened his mouth wide and snapped Johnny-Cake between his sharp teeth. Then, he rolled his foxy eyes and licked his lips.

Don't brag about what you can do. You can't outfox a fox.

Storytelling Tips

◉ Invite the listeners to join you in repeating Johnny-Cake's phrase, "I outran the little boy, the little old woman and the little old man, and I can outrun you, too-oo-o!"

◉ Encourage the listeners to cheer Johnny-Cake on by saying, "Run, Johnny, run!"

◉ Use different voices for Bear (who growls), Wolf (who snarls), and Fox (who sounds cagey).

Questions

◉ Does this story remind you of any other stories? Which ones?

◉ Did you think Bear would catch Johnny-Cake?

◉ Did you think Wolf would catch Johnny-Cake?

◉ What do you think a Johnny-Cake is? (Johnny-Cake is like cornbread, only it is round.)

DIFFERENT AND ALIKE

The Gingerbread Boy And Johnny Cake	
How Alike	How Different

Materials

two stories—one of "Johnny-Cake" and one of "The Gingerbread Boy" · paper markers

Steps

◉ After telling "Johnny-Cake," tell or read the story of "The Gingerbread Boy."

◉ Discuss how the two stories are alike and different.

◉ Write the comments on a chart.

ROUND IS TASTIEST

Materials

Cornmeal or cornbread mix • eggs • shortening or vegetable oil • skillet or muffin tins • milk • glasses

Steps

Note: Use caution when handling hot pans. Check for possible food allergies.

◉ Read the directions on the back of the package. Johnny-Cake is a flat cornbread. If baking cornbread from cornmeal, skip the step of adding the baking powder to make a flat bread.

◉ Serve the Johnny-Cake hot with a cold glass of milk.

◉ Retell the story while the listeners are enjoying the Johnny-Cake.

The Flying Contest
or How Kunibre Became King of the Birds

BASED ON A FOLKTALE FROM
SURINAME, THIS STORY IS ABOUT A
FLYING CONTEST TO DETERMINE WHO
WOULD BECOME THE KING OF THE
BIRDS AND HOW ONE BIRD
OUTSMARTS THEM ALL.

Once long ago, the birds came together and decided that they must have a king. The Lion was the king of the animals that walked on the earth, but the birds wanted to have their own king to rule over the skies. So the birds all went to Lion and asked him to call a meeting of all the birds.

Pretend to bow to a king.

The council of all the birds came together to decide who should be king. Lion asked the birds how they wanted to settle who should be king. The birds thought and thought, but they didn't know how to decide who should be king. As they talked, Falcon wanted to suggest that they decide who should be king by who could fly the highest. Falcon knew that he could fly the highest, but he did not want the other birds to think that he thought he should be king. Kunibre said that he should be king because even though he was the smallest bird, he was smart.

Flap your arms like wings.

Nightingale said, "I could suggest a contest to be decided by singing, but I am the best singer. If I sing a note, then I shall be king. We need a way that is fair to settle this contest. Since God gave us all wings, I suggest that the bird who flies the highest should be king."

Hearing this, Falcon was delighted. He knew that he could fly the highest. He said, "Yes, I think that is fair."

Kunibre jumped up and said, "Yes, I think this is the best plan. Whoever can fly the highest should be king."

Then, quickly and secretly, Kunibre flew onto the back of Falcon while Falcon was not watching. Kunibre was so light that Falcon did not feel him on his back as he soared higher and higher into the sky.

When all the birds landed, they said, "Falcon flew the highest, so Falcon shall be named our king." Then they noticed Kunibre on top of Falcon's back. They said, "No, Kunibre has flown higher than Falcon. Kunibre, the smart one, shall be our king."

Use your special abilities to do what you do best.

Storytelling Tips

🌀 Describe Kunibre as a very small bird, much like a sparrow or a finch.

🌀 Extend your arms and fly like a bird, showing how Falcon flew higher and higher into the sky.

🌀 Use a deep, wise voice for Lion. Use a medium voice for Nightingale. Use a small but confident voice for Kunibre. Use a proud voice for Falcon.

Questions

🌀 Why didn't Falcon simply say that he wanted to be king of the birds?

🌀 Do you think that Nightingale wanted to be king? Why?

🌀 Have you ever had a time when, even though you were the smallest, you had an idea as good as those of the adults in your family? What was your idea?

BIRD KINGS

Materials

Poster board and markers or paper and pencils

Steps

◉ Remind the listeners of the birds in the story (Kunibre, Falcon, and Nightingale).

◉ Write the names of the birds or draw pictures of them on the paper or poster board.

◉ Ask the listeners to name other kinds of birds. Would any of them make a good bird king? Why?

◉ Write the names of the birds or draw pictures on the paper or poster board.

USING YOUR WITS

UNIQUE BIRDS

Materials

Paper and pencils or poster board and markers

Steps

◉ Write the names of the three birds in the story on a sheet of paper or poster board.

◉ Invite the listeners to describe each of the birds.

◉ Under the name of each bird, write the words used to describe the bird, such as, "Kunibre—small, smart, king."

Kunibre	Falcon	Nightingale

WHAT DO I DO WELL?

" What I Do Well "

Jackie P.

Materials

Drawing paper • crayons or markers

Steps

⦿ Talk about how each bird in the story had a special talent. Kunibre was smart. Nightingale could sing well. Falcon could fly high.

⦿ Encourage the children to draw a picture showing something they do well.

⦿ Discuss the pictures and encourage the listeners to name other things that each person does well.

The Great Game in the Sky

MANY YEARS AGO, THE ANIMALS OF THE WOODS AND FORESTS HAD A GREAT ARGUMENT. IT HAPPENED SO LONG AGO THAT NO ONE KNOWS FOR SURE WHY THEY ARGUED, BUT TO SETTLE IT, THEY DECIDED TO PLAY A GAME OF LACROSSE.

The animals laid out the playing field with one end to the North, the other to the South. When the playing field was finished, the animals chose the teams they would play on. On the North side were the animals with fur (Bear, Deer, Wolf, Otter, Raccoon, Beaver, Rabbit, and Squirrel, to name a few). On the South side were the animals with feathers (Eagle, Hawk, Duck, Stork, Gull, Crow, Blue Jay, and Sparrow, to name a few).

Spread your arms to indicate a large playing field.

Suddenly, a soft small voice said, "Which side is mine, North or South?"

All of the animals stopped and looked at the tiny, mysterious creature.

Look amazed.

The animals with fur said, "You can't be on our side, you have wings and you are so small."

The animals with feathers said, "You can't be on our side, you have no feathers."

The strong voice of Otter rang out above the other voices. "No one who wants to play should be left out," he said.

Speak in a strong voice.

All the animals agreed. They made a tiny lacrosse stick for the tiny, mysterious creature and let him join the animals-with-fur team. The tiny, mysterious creature crawled onto Otter's back to have a better view.

Then the game began. All the animals with fur lined up on the North side, with Bear and Deer in front, followed by Wolf, Otter, Raccoon, Beaver, Rabbit, and Squirrel (to name a few who lived on earth). All the animals with wings lined up on the South side, with Eagle and Hawk

Put hands on hips and stomp on the ground.

in front, followed by Duck, Stork, Gull, Crow, Blue Jay, and Sparrow (to name a few who flew in the sky).

Flap arms like wings.

When the ball was tossed, Deer grabbed it and ran toward the goal. Before Deer could reach the goal, Stork flew down and got the ball from Deer. Wolf used the lacrosse stick to get the ball back and tossed it to Beaver, but Hawk flew down and stole the ball.

Pretend to toss a ball around.

The animals tried to reach Hawk, but he flew too high in the sky.

The birds passed the ball from player to player as they flew toward the northern goal, just out of the reach of the animals. The birds played and played in the sky until it was almost sunset.

All of a sudden, as the sky began to darken, the tiny, mysterious creature flew into the group of birds playing with the ball. In a split second, the tiny, mysterious creature seized the ball from the startled birds and flew toward the southern goal, keeping away from the birds. As it flew across the southern goal line the animals with fur shouted and cheered, "We won, we won, the animals with fur won!"

Look surprised.

When the tiny, mysterious creature returned to earth, the animals asked, "What is your name?"

"My name is Bat," replied the tiny, mysterious creature.

"You are the littlest and the best player," said the animals. "You shall have a special gift."

Bat's gift, for then and for always, was to sleep all day. Then at night, while the animals slept, Bat would be able to catch and eat all the tasty insects that come out at night.

Bat is still collecting his reward for being the littlest and best lacrosse player of all.

Size makes no difference. Everyone counts!

Storytelling Tips

🌀 Explain that lacrosse is a game that is played with a racket, like tennis, except that the racket head is made to catch the ball and then throw it. If possible, have a lacrosse racket and ball to show to the children.

🌀 Use a wise-sounding voice for Otter.

🌀 Vary the tone and speed of your voice to match the events in the story. For example, speak in an excited voice when you tell about the game and the ball being tossed from one player to the other. Speak in a disappointed voice when the animals with fur think that they will lose the game because no one can reach the ball with the birds playing in the sky.

Questions

🌀 How do you feel when you are told that you are too little to play a game with bigger kids?

🌀 How do you feel when you are told that you are too little to do a chore?

🌀 What do you wish the bigger kids would say to you?

🌀 What do you wish your parents would say to you?

WHAT IS LACROSSE?

Materials

Lacrosse racket and
ball • tennis racket
and ball • or pictures
of each item (a
sports equipment
catalog is a good
place to look)

Steps

◉ Show the two rackets and ask how the lacrosse racket is like a
tennis racket and how is it different.

◉ Show a lacrosse ball and a tennis ball. Ask how the lacrosse ball is
like a tennis ball and how it is different?

◉ Explain that a lacrosse match has goal lines, like a soccer or
hockey match.

STORY SIGNALS

Materials

Small drum • mallet

Steps

⊚ Start playing the drum with a rhythm that is inviting. Try quick, tapping sounds.

⊚ As the listeners come to investigate what they are hearing, tell them the story they heard is from a Native American Tribe, the Menominee (Me-nom-i-nee).

⊚ Explain that the Menominee people lived in areas where there are woodlands and that they used drums as a way of sending messages.

⊚ Play the drum for a while, making up rhythms.

⊚ Use the drum to signal the start of the story and then at the story's climax. If you are very comfortable playing the drum, use it to accompany your story, or invite a friend to play and use the rhythm of the drum to set the tone of the story.

FUR OR FEATHERS?

Materials

Large sheets of paper or poster board • two colors of markers

Fur	Feathers

Steps

◉ Discuss the two teams in the story, the animals with fur and the animals with feathers.

◉ Draw a long line down the middle of the paper or poster board.

◉ Write "fur" at the top of the first column and "feathers" at the top of the second column.

◉ Recall all the animals in the story. After each is named, write the animal name in the appropriate column.

◉ Using the other marker, ask the listeners to think of additional animals that could go in each column.

◉ Ask where "Bat" should go. According to the story, it goes in both. Write Bat in both columns or print it across both columns.

Appreciating Differences

Big City Mouse, Small Town Mouse

A BIG CITY MOUSE AND SMALL TOWN
MOUSE TRADE PLACES AND FIND THEIR
NEW HOMES ARE JUST WHAT THEY ALWAYS
WANTED IN THIS STORY INSPIRED BY
AESOP'S FABLE.

Once upon a time, there was a great gleaming city, teeming with people, cars, taxis, and buses. In this great gleaming city, there lived a mouse, a big city mouse. He had lived in little apartments, big tenement buildings, and huge skyscrapers, but always in the city. Now he lived in a penthouse, a luxurious penthouse with a view of a famous park out one window and a view of a busy street corner out another window.

Stretch your arms up high to show how big the buildings in the city are.

Every evening at sunset, Big City Mouse stood before the big picture window and stared out at dusk descending on the lovely park below. He wished for someone, anyone, to share the view with him. He had no one to tell about the colors of the sunset.

No one was around to hear him say how his day had gone or help him plan for tomorrow. Big City Mouse was a very lonely mouse.

Big City Mouse loved cheese, especially the kinds of hard cheese wrapped in little foils of paper. When he nibbled and nibbled the cheese, there was no one to tell about the different flavors or to say which one was best. One of the packages of cheese was from France. It had a picture of the Eiffel Tower on the front of the package. Big City Mouse was nibbling on the hard cheese and staring down at the busy traffic below. The cars were speeding by. The taxis were careening around the corners. One taxi ran a red light and almost hit a fat cat crossing the street. Big City Mouse even felt sorry for the cat. Big City Mouse was a very lonely mouse.

Pretend to nibble cheese.

One day, Big City Mouse returned from shopping feeling completely exhausted. He had spent all day trying to get to all the best shops in the city. He had dodged speeding cars and giant buses. Big City Mouse was so relieved to get out of the traffic and back to his penthouse that he dropped all his packages right in the middle of the floor. He did not even unpack them. He had no one to show all the new things he had bought. Big City Mouse was a very lonely mouse.

Pretend to open a letter.

Just then the doorman brought a special letter to Big City Mouse. It was an invitation that read,

"Come to Small Town Upstate for a Family Reunion. All your cousins from far and wide will be there for a picnic in the meadow. Please come." Big City Mouse thought of all the cousins from far and wide and decided he must go.

Meanwhile, Small Town Mouse, who lived in Small Town, was sitting on his back porch, looking out at the meadow. His back porch was a perfect place to sit and watch the sunset. The sunlight glowed as it descended on the golden grasses. The rays of the sun twinkled as the sun set behind the little hill.

Pretend to rock in a rocking chair.

Everyone in Small Town said Small Town Mouse had the best place in town for looking at the sunset. Every day all the neighborhood mice from up and down the only street in town came to sit on Small Town Mouse's back porch. They watched the sunset. They gossiped about what was happening at the firehouse, the school house, the church house, and the cottage cheese-making shop. Small Town Mouse could not enjoy the beautiful sunset with all those chattering mice. Small Town Mouse went into his house, put his paws over his ears and said, "I cannot listen any more. I am tired of having all these people at my house every day." Small town mouse was a very frustrated mouse.

Small Town Mouse longed for a meal of fancy cheeses. Instead, he had cottage cheese with tomatoes, cottage cheese with squash, cottage cheese with green beans, and cottage cheese with corn.

He thought of all the fancy hard cheeses from around the world. He remembered seeing one cheese wrapped in foil with a picture of the Eiffel Tower on the package. Small Town Mouse said, "I am tired of having only cottage cheese to eat every day." Small Town Mouse was a very frustrated mouse.

Small Town Mouse was just about to send the chattering neighbors home so he could enjoy the last rays of the sunset in peace. Then, "Swoop, swoop, swoop," everyone from the back porch scurried in every direction, running to their homes. Small Town Mouse knew that swooping sound. It was the swooping wings of a big owl, swooping around the corner of Small Town Mouse's house. Small Town Mouse was relieved that not only had the owl gone, but all his mice neighbors had also gone home. But, there on his back porch were all the little bowls of cottage cheese they had brought with them to eat while they watched the sunset across the meadow. Small Town Mouse said, "I am tired of cleaning up this mess every day." Small Town Mouse was a very frustrated mouse.

Encourage the listeners to join you in saying, "The Small Town Mouse was a very frustrated mouse."

Flap arms like wings.

Hold up
imaginary
letter.

Then he saw a letter lying on the porch. It was addressed to him. Someone must have dropped it while escaping the owl. Small Town Mouse read the letter. It said, "Come to Small Town for a Family Reunion. All your cousins from far and wide will be there for a picnic in the meadow. Please come." Small Town Mouse thought of all the cousins from far and wide and decided he must go. He would not have far to go. It would be in the meadow, just behind his house. He remembered his Big City cousin he met at the last family reunion. He wanted to ask Big City Mouse about the skyscrapers and pent-houses. He wanted to ask him about the big buses and trucks. He wanted to ask him about riding in a fast taxi and careening around the corners. Small Town Mouse also wanted to ask his big city cousin about the Eiffel Tower hard cheese.

Pretend to
nibble cheese.

On the day of the reunion, the two mouse cousins shared a table. Big City Mouse shared a basket of hard cheeses from all over the world. Small Town Mouse shared a bowl of cottage cheese with succotash, a mixture of all the best vegetables from his garden.

Big City Mouse talked about his life in the big city. He said he was a very lonely mouse in the big city. Small Town Mouse could not believe his ears. The big city sounded just like the exciting place where he had always dreamed of living.

Then, Small Town Mouse told of his life in this small town. He said he was very tired of everything in this small town with only one street. Big City Mouse could not believe his ears. The small town sounded just like the peaceful place where he had always dreamed of living.

Wise Old Mouse overheard them and said, "If you don't like your life, then change it." And so they did. They swapped places. Small Town Mouse moved to the big city, and Big City Mouse moved to the small town.

And do you know, each year at the family reunion, Big City Mouse and Small Town Mouse run to each other and dance and hug. The small town is just the kind of place that Big City Mouse has always dreamed of living. He is not lonely anymore. He has a back porch filled with gossiping neighbors, eating their bowls of cottage cheese with garden vegetables. There is not a single car in sight when he crosses the street. Best of all, there is no screeching taxi cab, only the occasional swooping owl, careening around the corner of the house.

Dance and skip.

Big City Mouse is no longer a very lonely mouse; he has become a small town mouse.

For Small Town Mouse, the big city is just the most exciting place. It is just the kind of place that Small Town Mouse always dreamed of living. He has a penthouse view of a lush green park from one window and a view of the traffic from another. There are no gossiping neighbors from down the street to disturb him while he enjoys the views. He savors the hard cheeses from the penthouse pantry. He loves the sound of the bustling traffic that never stops. Best of all, there is no swooping owl, only the occasional screeching taxi, careening around the corner. Small Town Mouse is no longer a very frustrated mouse. He lives in an exciting city; he has become a big city mouse.

The two mouse cousins always look forward to the family reunion each year. They like hearing Wise Old Mouse say, "See, I told you: If you don't like your life, then change it."

At each family reunion, the two mouse cousins talk about how lucky they are to live in their new places. They each nibble cheese from a little foil package with a picture of the Eiffel Tower on the front. They are glad they listened to the advice of Wise Old Mouse.

You won't know if you like something unless you try it.

Storytelling Tips

- Tell about the characteristics of Big City life at a hurried pace. Tell about Small Town life at a slow pace and pause often, speaking in a leisurely way.

- Add drama and sound effects at the sound of the "screech, screech, screech of the taxi cab careening around the corner" and "swoop, swoop, swoop of the owl flying around the corner."

- Add gestures at appropriate places. For example, clasp your hands over your ears when Small Town Mouse cannot stand to hear those chattering mice a minute longer. Look for other places to use gestures, such as drooped shoulders when describing Big City Mouse as one lonely mouse.

- Say, "Big City Mouse was a very lonely mouse," in a sad voice and "Small Town Mouse was a very frustrated mouse," in an exasperated voice. Repeat these phrases more often, if you like.

Questions

- Before the story, ask, "What do you like about where you live? Is it a big city, the country, a small town?"

- After the story, ask, "Where would you like to live if you could move?"

LONELY AND FRUSTRATED

Materials

Full-length mirror

Steps

◉ Invite the listeners to look in the mirror and show what Big City Mouse might look like when he says, "I am a very lonely mouse."

◉ Next, have them look in the mirror and show what Small Town Mouse might look like when he says, "I am a very frustrated mouse."

◉ Encourage two listeners to pantomime the two mice eating the cottage cheese with a spoon and nibbling on hard cheese.

◉ Ask one listener to pantomime what happens at a family reunion or gathering where families are seeing relatives they have not seen in a long time.

COMPARISON DRAWING

Materials

Drawing paper • markers or crayons

Steps

◉ Fold a large sheet of paper down the middle.

◉ Draw a scene from the Big City on the left side and the Small Town on the right side.

◉ Younger children can draw a Big City Mouse and Small Town Mouse. Ask them to put at least one thing in the picture that will let the viewer know that one picture represents the Big City and the other the Small Town.

◉ Label each side of the picture. Older children can dictate a phrase for you to write on their picture or write the description themselves.

TASTING CHEESES

Materials

Variety of hard cheeses (some in foil-wrapped packages) • cottage cheese • cutting board and knife • small bowls or cups • spoons, napkins • fruit or fruit juice

Steps

Note: Check for food allergies before offering cheese to taste.

◉ Mention that Big City Mouse and Small Town Mouse enjoyed different cheeses. Ask the listeners which kinds of cheese each mouse liked.

◉ If possible, allow the listeners to examine cheese sampler packages, which are wrapped in foil.

◉ Everyone can taste the hard cheeses and the cottage cheese. Cut the cheeses into small nibble-sized versions, much like the mice would eat. Put the cottage cheese in small bowls or cups. Make sure the children know the names of the cheeses.

◉ Provide slices of fruit or fruit juice to accompany the tasting party.

"Could Be Worse!"

By James Stevenson

THIS VARIATION OF A YIDDISH FOLKTALE IS THE STORY OF A GRANDFATHER WHO DOES EVERYTHING THE SAME WAY EVERY DAY. HE HEARS HIS GRANDCHILDREN TALKING ABOUT HIS BORING LIFE, SO HE TELLS THEM AN EXCITING STORY ABOUT HIS ADVENTURES.

At Grandpa's house things were always the same. Grandpa always had the same thing for breakfast. Every day he read the paper.

Use a special voice and inflection.

And he always said the same thing, no matter what. "Could be worse."

"Grandpa! That awful dog ate this sofa cushion!"

Use a special voice and inflection.

"Could be worse."

"I got a splinter in my finger, Grandpa."

"Could be worse."

"My bike has a flat and my sneakers have a hole and I lost my kite in a tree, Grandpa."

"Could be worse."

(One day Grandpa overheard the children talking outside his window.)

Place your hand behind your ear.

Mary Ann said, "How come Grandpa never says anything interesting?"

"I guess it's because nothing interesting happens to him," said Louie.

Next morning at breakfast Grandpa said something different.

He said, "Guess what! Last night, when I was asleep, a large bird pulled me out of bed and took me for a long ride and dropped me in the mountains.

Use an excited voice.

I heard a noise. It was an abominable snowman with a huge snowball which he threw at me.

I got stuck inside the snowball, which rolled down the mountain.

It finally landed on the desert and began to melt.

I walked across the desert.

Suddenly I heard footsteps coming nearer and nearer.

A moment later I got squished by a giant something-or-other.

Make heavy steps.

Before I could get up, I heard a strange noise.

A great blob of marmalade was coming toward me.

It chased me across the desert until I crashed into something tall. It was sort of like an ostrich and very cross.

It gave me a big kick. I went up into some storm clouds, almost got hit by lightning, fell out of the clouds, and landed in an ocean.

I sank down about a mile to the bottom. I saw an enormous goldfish coming at me.

Make loud splashing noises.

I swam away as fast as I could and hid under a cup that had air in it.

When it was safe, I crawled out. I started to walk, but my foot got stuck in the grip of a gigantic lobster.

Make swimming motions with your arms.

I didn't know what to do.

But just then a big squid came along and squirted black ink all over the lobster.

I escaped and hitched a ride on a sea turtle that was

going to the top for a bit of sunshine.

I was fortunate to find a piece of toast floating by and rode to shore, where I discovered a newspaper.

Make swimming motions with your arms.

I quickly folded it into an airplane and flew across the sea and back home to bed.

Now, what do you think of that?"

Pause.

"Could be worse!" said the children.

This is the text of the story "*Could be Worse!*" by James Stevenson.

Everyone has interesting stories to share.

APPRECIATING DIFFERENCES

Storytelling Tips

- Describe a typical day in the grandfather's life, emphasizing the sameness of his days.

- Practice repeating the phrase "Could be worse," using a "grandfather's voice and the same inflection.

- In the section where the grandfather tells his exciting story, it is not necessary to repeat the exact events included in the text. The happenings can be adjusted to match the children who are listening and expanded to follow their interests, recent events in their lives, or the people and geography of your area.

- Vary the pace of the story to match the message being conveyed. The first part is slow and methodical. During the grandfather's story speed up the tempo of the phrases to demonstrate excitement.

Questions

- Why did the children think the grandfather's life was boring?

- Why was the grandfather's story so exciting?

- What part of the grandfather's story did you like best?

SOUND SYMBOLS

Materials

none required

Steps

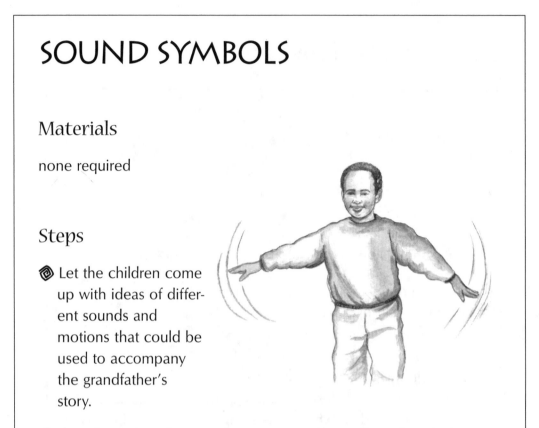

- Let the children come up with ideas of different sounds and motions that could be used to accompany the grandfather's story.

- Together select the sounds or motions that will work with the story. For example:

  Flap wings for the bird carrying the grandfather.

  Make circular motions with hands for rolling down the mountain.

  Rub hands on thighs for walking across the desert.

  Retell the story with the children's suggestions for sounds and motions. Together make the sounds and/or motions that support the story.

- Reflect on the story with the sounds and motions. Did they make the story better? Could you use different sounds?

APPRECIATING SENIOR CITIZENS

Materials

tape recorder and camera

Steps

◉ Set up a visit with a grandparent or senior citizen.

◉ Write down questions that the children would like to ask during the visit.

◉ Together interview the grandparent or older friend.

◉ Ask the grandparent or older friend to tell a story about something exciting that happened to them.

◉ Tape record the story as it is being told.

◉ Take a picture of the older storyteller.

◉ Store the picture and the tape together so they can be used again.

Monkey's and Rabbit's Bad Habits

MONKEY AND RABBIT ARE FRIENDS, BUT THEY HAVE ANNOYING HABITS. THIS FUNNY STORY, BASED ON A WEST AFRICAN TALE, IS ABOUT THEIR ATTEMPT TO BREAK THEIR BAD HABITS FOR A DAY.

Monkey and Rabbit were sitting on the river bank talking. Rabbit liked to listen to Monkey, except for one small problem: Rabbit was often distracted from what Monkey was saying by Monkey's scratching. Monkey talked and scratched, scratched and talked. He scratched the top of his head. He scratched his hairy chin. He scratched his left arm, then he scratched his right.

Scratch the top of your head, your chin, your left arm, then your right.

Monkey liked talking with Rabbit, except for one small problem. Monkey was often distracted from what Rabbit was saying by Rabbit's sniffing and twitching and flopping. Rabbit sniffed the air, twitched her nose, and flopped her ears from side to side. She sniffed and twitched and flopped, and flopped and twitched and sniffed.

Sniff, twitch your nose, then turn your head from side to side.

Finally, Monkey said, "Will you stop that?"

"Stop what?" asked Rabbit.

"Stop that sniffing the air, twitching your nose, and flopping those long ears," said Monkey.

"All that sniffing, twitching, and flopping is driving me crazy. What a bad habit you have!"

"What a bad habit I have? What about you? All the time you are talking to me, you are scratching. First, you scratch the top of your head. Then, you scratch your chin. Next, you scratch your left arm, then your right. You are always scratching. What a bad habit you have!"

Scratch the top of your head, your chin, your left arm, then your right

"Well, I don't have to scratch. I can stop scratching anytime I want," said Monkey.

"Well, I don't have to sniff and twitch and flop," said Rabbit. "I can stop sniffing and twitching and flopping anytime I want."

Then Monkey challenged Rabbit to a contest. "Let's just see. I know I can go all day without scratching, if you can go all day without sniffing and twitching and flopping. It is morning now. If we can be still all day until the sun sets, we can break these bad habits."

So, Monkey sat very still.

And Rabbit sat very still.

Keep your body very still with your arms straight down at your sides.

Neither moved a muscle, but Monkey's skin itched so much. He wanted to scratch the top of his head. He did so want to scratch his hairy chin. His left arm itched, and his right arm itched, but Monkey sat very still.

Keep your body very still with your arms straight down at your sides.

Rabbit also did not move a muscle, but Rabbit did so want to sniff the air for danger. She thought she smelled a lion in the grass, but she did not sniff and twitch her nose. She did not twitch, and she did not flop her ears from side to side to listen for danger. Rabbit sat very still.

Finally, Rabbit said, "Monkey, I have an idea. We've been sitting here very still for a very long time. I'm getting bored. Let's tell stories to pass the time of day."

"Fine, idea, Rabbit, why don't you tell the first story."

So, Rabbit began, "Just yesterday as I was coming down to the river bank to visit with you, I thought I smelled a lion in the grass. So, I sniffed, sniffed, sniffed the air, but there was no lion there. Just to be sure, I twitched my nose several times, but there was no lion there. Then, I flopped my ears and listened, but there was no lion there. I was so relieved that there was no danger. Then I continued to the river bank to see you, my friend."

Sniff, twitch your nose, then turn your head from side to side.

Monkey, noticing how Rabbit had managed to sneak in some sniffing, twitching, and flopping into her story, decided to tell a story of his own.

Monkey said, "Just yesterday on my way down to the river bank to visit with you, I passed some children. One child threw a coconut and hit me on my head, right here. Another boy threw a coconut shell and hit me on my chin, right here. Two girls threw coconut shells at me and hit me on each arm. Then I ran as fast as I could to the river bank to see you, my friend."

Scratch the top of your head, your chin, your left arm, then your right.

Rabbit began to giggle. Monkey started to laugh. Rabbit knew what Monkey was doing, and Monkey knew what Rabbit was doing.

"Well, that's a good story, but you lose the contest, Monkey. You scratched all through your story," said Rabbit.

"Well, that was a good story, Rabbit, but you sniffed and twitched and flopped all through your story," said Monkey.

Sniff, twitch your nose, then turn your head from side to side.

"I guess neither one of us can be still all day," said Rabbit. "I just can't break this bad habit," she said as she sniffed the air for danger, twitched her nose, and flopped her ears.

MONKEY'S AND RABBITS BAD HABITS

Scratch the top of your head, your chin, your left arm, then your right.

"Neither can I," said Monkey as he scratched the top of his head, scratched his hairy chin, and scratched his left arm, then his right.

Bad habits are hard to break, they agreed, and to this day, Monkey still scratches, and Rabbit still sniffs and twitches and flops.

Appreciate your friends, even if they have some annoying habits.

Storytelling Tips

◉ Encourage the listeners to join you in making the movements of scratching Monkey and sniffing, twitching, flopping Rabbit.

◉ Experiment with two different voices for the characters. Say Monkey's words in a high-pitched, excited voice and Rabbit's in a soft, gentle voice.

◉ Let one group of listeners do Monkey's movements and another group do Rabbit's movements.

Questions

◉ Do you have any habits you are trying to break? Have you been successful at breaking the habit? How did you do it?

◉ What habits do you have? Are they good habits or are they bad habits?

MONKEY'S & RABBIT'S CONTEST

Materials

None needed

Steps

◉ Have a contest to
see who can sit still
longer, Monkey or
Rabbit. One child or
group can be
Monkey, and another
child or group can be
Rabbit. The story-
teller can also be
Monkey or Rabbit.

◉ Try sitting very still.

◉ After someone
moves talk about how it is easier for some people to be still than
others. Discuss a time when you found it difficult to sit still.

STICK PUPPETS

Materials

Crayons or markers • poster board or stiff paper popsicle sticks or tongue depressors • scissors • stapler

Steps

◉ Draw your own monkey or rabbit face, or copy one. Younger children may need help.

◉ Cut out the faces of the monkey and the rabbit.

◉ Staple the faces onto popsicle sticks or tongue depressors.

◉ Retell the story, holding up the stick puppets as each character is speaking.

◉ Use stuffed animals as a variation.

The Woman Who Wanted More Noise

IN THIS RETOLD STORY, A CITY WOMAN
WHO MOVES TO THE COUNTRY FINDS
THAT IT IS TOO QUIET, SO SHE BRINGS
ANIMALS, A NOISY CAR, AND FINALLY
CHILDREN TO HER FARM SO THERE IS
LOTS OF GOOD NOISE.

APPRECIATING DIFFERENCES

Once there was a woman who

lived in the city. She had lived in the city all of her life and she loved the city sounds. She liked the streetcars, big trucks, and buses. She liked the sounds of many people as they moved along the streets and stores. She loved the city sounds.

One day the woman received a letter in the mail from her cousin who lived in the country. Her cousin wrote, "I am moving to Australia. You can have my farm in the country." The city woman thought that the farm would be a fine place to live so she moved from her city home to the country.

When she arrived in the country she found that her new home was beautiful. There was plenty of land around the house; it had an apple orchard, a big red barn, and a large garden.

But the woman had a problem: she couldn't go to sleep at night. It was too quiet in the country. She missed all the sounds of the city.

She went to see her neighbor who lived on a farm not far away. She asked the neighbor, "What can I do to get some noise on my farm? I can't sleep at night, because it is too quiet." The neighbor suggested that she buy some animals that made noises. She hurried out to buy a cow. She brought the cow home and put her in the big red barn. The cow made a fine noise, but it was not enough.

Moo like a cow.

So she bought a dog. She put the dog in the yard and fed him well. The dog made a fine noise, but it was not enough.

Bark like a dog.

Meow like a cat.

So she bought a cat. She put the cat in her house so she could hear her meow. The cat made a fine noise, but it was not enough.

Quack like a duck.

So she bought some ducks. She put the ducks in her pond beside her garden. The ducks made a fine noise, but it was not enough.

So she bought hens, a rooster, and little chicks. She put the hens, rooster, and little chicks in a coop next to the barn. They made a fine noise, but it was not enough.

Crow like a rooster.

Oink like a pig.

So she bought a pig. The pig made a fine noise, but it was not enough.

She still couldn't go to sleep at night; it was too quiet. The woman wanted more noise on her farm, so she decided to buy an old broken down car with a loud horn. The woman would drive the old broken down car around the farm and blow the horn loudly. It made a fine noise. When it was too quiet the woman would go to her car and honk the horn. All the animals would make their sounds. All together they made a very loud noise, but it was not enough noise.

Honk like a car horn.

At night the woman could not sleep because she missed the sounds of the city. The woman tried to figure out what other sounds she was missing from the city. What sounds would make her happy in the country? The woman decided what was missing. It was children!

Ask the listeners to make a happy noise.

So, she went to the city and found children who would come and visit her farm. She found many boys and girls who wanted to come to play on her farm. They were very noisy. They made a fine noise.

APPRECIATING DIFFERENCES

Now the animals would make their sounds, the woman would honk the car horn, and the children would play. Now there were many sounds: the cow, the dog, the cat, the ducks, the hen and rooster, the pig, the horn of the old car, and all the children.

Now it was **not** quiet. It was not quiet at all; it was very noisy.

The woman was very happy because now there was enough noise. She loved the farm, and she could go to sleep at night with all the beautiful sounds of the country.

Pretend to go to sleep.

What seems noisy to one person may seem quiet to another.

Storytelling Tips

◉ Before telling the story, talk about some of the sounds that might be heard in the city and on a farm. Many young children have limited experiences in these two very different environments.

◉ Practice using consistent sounds for each item added to the story. Determine how you can repeat the sounds so that children can hear the cumulative items of the story. Young listeners will let you know if you have left out one of the sounds when you are retelling the story.

◉ Encourage the listeners to make the sounds of the cow, dog, cat, ducks, hen, rooster and little chicks, pig, old broken-down car, and children when you say "they all made good noise."

◉ Ask one listener or a small group to make one specific sound, such as "moo, moo" for the cow. The listeners would make their specific noise at the appropriate time, and again at the end of the story when all the sounds are repeated together.

◉ Use a consistent signal to let the listeners know when they are to join in the telling. It can be a phrase such as "the pig made a fine noise," "the cat made a fine noise," "they all made a fine noise" or a hand signal. If the listeners have trouble knowing when to make the sounds, pause and repeat the signal.

Questions

◉ What might have happened if the woman had always lived in the country and had to move to the city?

◉ Why did the woman like all the noise and think it was good noise?

◉ What sounds do you like to hear?

APPRECIATING DIFFERENCES

HONK IF YOU LIVE ON A FARM

Materials

A book about farm animals that could be found on the farm

Steps

◉ Read the book.

◉ Discuss and make the sounds of the animals that are pictured in the book.

◉ Retell the story and add animals from the book to a new oral version of the "The Woman Who Wanted More Noise."

◉ Talk about other sounds you might hear on a farm, such as those made by equipment.

LISTENING WALK

Materials

paper and markers

Steps

◉ Talk about some of the sounds that might be heard outside.

◉ Take the listeners for a walk outside and listen for all kinds of sounds.

◉ Come back inside and talk about the sounds you heard on the walk.

◉ Write down some of the sounds you heard.

◉ With the listeners' help, create a map of the walk and the sounds heard along the way.

APPRECIATING DIFFERENCES

SOUND DRAMA

Materials

None needed

Steps

- Invite each listener, one at a time, to make a sound.

- The others try to guess what the sound is and where one might hear it.

- If a listener is hesitant about making a sound, let him participate in just the guessing part.

The Lost Mitten With Tiny, ShinyBeads

IN THIS VERSION OF A UKRAINIAN
FOLKTALE, A LITTLE BOY LOSES HIS
WARM MITTEN IN THE FOREST.
THE TALE IS THE STORY OF WHAT
HAPPENS WHEN ANIMALS CRAWL
INSIDE THE MITTEN TO KEEP WARM.

Once upon a time a grandmother and her grandson lived together in a little house beside a great woods. One cold winter morning, the grandmother said, "Grandson, please go and find some kindling for the fire, so that I might make some porridge."

The boy, being an obedient boy, dressed in his warmest winter snowsuit. He pulled on his fur-lined boots. He wrapped his warm scarf around his neck. He pulled his warm hat over his ears. Then, he put on his mittens.

Pretend to put on a snowsuit, boots, a scarf, a hat, and mittens.

The mittens were ones his grandmother had made for him. She knitted them, stitched in warm fur, and sewed tiny, shiny beads on the outside. The boy loved his beautiful mittens.

He planned to fill his sled with kindling from the forest. Even with the howling wind, the swirling snow, and the gray skies, he liked walking in the woods.

The snow was so deep that it was difficult to find the little broken branches or to find the spot where the woodcutter often left scraps of wood. The boy pulled his sled deeper and deeper into the forest searching for the kindling. Each piece of kindling he found he put on his little sled.

Once when the boy stopped to pick up a piece of kindling, he saw a beautiful icicle hanging from the bough of a majestic evergreen tree. The boy took off one of his mittens and laid it carefully onto the sled. He touched the icicle and a few drops of water melted onto his hand.

THE LOST MITTEN WITH TINY, SHINY BEADS

Pretend to pluck the icicle from the tree.

The icicle glistened in his hand. Just ahead, he spotted a place where the woodcutter had worked. There would be some kindling there. He rushed ahead, pulling his sled behind him. The little boy did not notice that his beautiful furry mitten, with tiny, shiny beads stitched on the outside, dropped from the sled and fell onto the snow.

When the boy reached the clearing, he picked up the small pieces of kindling the woodcutter had left behind. He was so busy that he did not notice that his beautiful furry mitten, with tiny, shiny beads stitched on the outside, was missing.

When the sled was loaded, he started back home. His hand felt cold. He stopped to get his mitten from the sled, but he could not find it.

He looked under each stick of kindling on the sled, but he could not find his beautiful furry mitten, with tiny, shiny beads stitched on the outside.

The boy looked for the beautiful mitten everywhere. The wind continued to howl, and the blowing snow made it hard to see. He could not even see the tracks from his sled. With a heavy heart, he realized that he could not find his beautiful furry mitten, with tiny, shiny beads stitched on the outside.

Hunch as though shivering with hands in pockets.

So, the little boy put his cold hand in his pocket and started for home. With the swirling snow and his search for his mitten, he had gotten off the path and did not know which way was home. He was cold and getting more frightened by the minute. Then he remembered some advice the woodcutter had given him: follow the tall row of evergreens that line the path. The little boy searched until he found the evergreens that lined the path and made his way back to the little house beside a great woods.

Pretend to trudge through snow.

Meanwhile, his beautiful furry mitten, with tiny, shiny beads stitched on the outside, lay upon the snow. It seems that the little boy was not the only one who was cold that morning. Field Mouse had been out searching for dried seeds, and he became very cold. He spied the beautiful furry mitten, with tiny, shiny beads stitched on the outside. Field Mouse wiggled inside and felt the warm fur. He decided that he would wait out the snow storm inside this beautiful furry mitten, with tiny, shiny beads stitched on the outside. Just as Field Mouse was about to take a little nap, he heard someone outside the mitten. "Croak, croak, it is so cold outside. Please, may I come in?"

Pretend to wiggle inside the mitten.

"Who is that croaking voice outside in the cold?" the warm field mouse asked. "It is I, Frog, and I am so cold." Field Mouse, recognizing the croaking voice of Frog, said, "Yes, of course, there is always room for one more." So, Frog hopped inside the beautiful furry mitten, with tiny, shiny beads stitched on the outside.

Pretend to hop inside the mitten.

Just as Field Mouse and Frog were about to take a little nap, they heard someone outside the mitten. "Hoot, hoot, it is so cold outside. Please may I come in?"

"Who is that hooting voice outside in the cold?" the warm field mouse and frog asked. "It is I, Owl, and I am so cold." Field Mouse and Frog, recognizing the hooting voice of Owl, said, "Yes, of course, there is always room for one more." So, Owl flew inside the beautiful furry mitten, with tiny, shiny beads stitched on the outside.

Pretend to fly inside the mitten.

Just as Field Mouse, Frog, and Owl were about to take a

THE LOST MITTEN WITH TINY, SHINY BEADS

little nap, they heard someone outside the mitten. "Sniff, sniff, it is so cold outside. Please may I come in?"

"Who is that sniffing voice outside in the cold?" asked the warm friends.

Pretend to hop inside the mitten.

"It is I, Rabbit, and I am so cold." Field Mouse, Frog, and Owl, recognizing the sniffing voice of Rabbit, said, "Yes, of course, there is always room for one more." So, Rabbit hopped inside the beautiful furry mitten with tiny, shiny beads stitched on the outside.

Just as Field Mouse, Frog, Owl, and Rabbit were snuggling up to take a little nap, they heard someone outside the mitten. "Growl, growl, it is so cold outside. Please may I come in?"

"Who is that growling voice outside in the cold?" asked the warm friends. "It is I, Fox, and I am so cold." Field Mouse, Frog, Owl, and Rabbit thought it was getting very crowded inside. But, recognizing the growling voice of Fox, said, "Yes, of course, there is always room for one more." So, Fox crowded inside the beautiful furry mitten, with tiny, shiny beads stitched on the outside.

Pretend to crowd inside the mitten.

Just as Field Mouse, Frog, Owl, Rabbit, and Fox were settling down trying to make room for each other inside the tight space, they heard another voice. "Snarl, snarl, it is so cold outside. Please may I come in?"

"Who is that snarly voice outside in the cold?" asked the warm friends. "It is I, Mountain Lion, and I am so cold." Field Mouse, Frog, Owl, Rabbit, and Fox yelled back, "No! It is too crowded in here. We can barely move. Mountain Lion, you are too big. You cannot come in."

Mountain Lion was very cold and he began to snarl, cry,

APPRECIATING DIFFERENCES

and shiver. "Friends," he begged. "Please make room for me. It is so cold outside that my paws are freezing." So the warm friends crunched closer and said, "Yes, of course, there is always room for one more." So Mountain Lion crawled inside. The mitten was stretching, and stretching, and stretching. Finally, he was inside. The beautiful furry mitten had stretched so big that most of the tiny, shiny beads had popped off the outside, but the friends were warm inside the very tight space.

Pretend to crawl inside the mitten.

Just as they were settling down in close company inside the mitten, they heard another voice. "Chirp, chirp, it is so cold outside. Please may I come in?"

"Who is that chirping voice outside in the cold?" asked the warm friends stuffed inside. "It is I, Cricket, and I am so cold." Field Mouse, Frog, Owl, Rabbit, Fox, and Mountain Lion thought, if we can get a great big mountain lion inside this beautiful fur-lined mitten, we can stretch it a little more to get a tiny cricket inside. So they said, "Yes, of course, there is always room for one more." So Field Mouse, Frog, Owl, Rabbit, Fox, and Mountain Lion drew in their breaths to make room for Cricket.

The beautiful fur-lined mitten stretched and stretched. This time, it stretched so far that the stitches holding it together broke, and the beautiful fur-lined mitten burst open.

Field Mouse, Frog, Owl, Rabbit, Fox, and Mountain Lion tumbled out onto the cold snow. While they had been inside, the wind had stopped blowing, and the sun was peeking through the clouds. So Field Mouse, Frog, Owl, Rabbit, Fox, and Mountain Lion felt the warmth of the sun and rushed back to their homes in the great woods.

THE LOST MITTEN WITH TINY, SHINY BEADS

Only cricket was left. Finding a piece of the beautiful furry mitten, with one tiny, shiny bead left on the outside, Cricket said, "This will make me a nice, warm home, to wait out the winter until the spring comes." And so he did.

One day the following spring, the little boy was playing along the path where the evergreens lead into the big woods, when he found a scrap of woven cloth. It reminded him of his beautiful furry mitten, with tiny, shiny beads stitched on the outside. In fact, there was one tiny, shiny bead stitched on the scrap of woven cloth. When he picked it up, he heard a voice inside.

"Chirp, chirp, who is moving my warm home?"

"It is I, Little Boy, who lives in the house beside the big woods. How did you come to have this scrap of woven cloth for your house?" asked the boy.

"Chirp, chirp, now that is a quite a story, chirp, chirp. Sit here on this stack of kindling and let me tell you about a cold day last winter."

So, Cricket hopped upon the shoulder of the little boy and told the story of how the beautiful furry mitten with tiny, shiny beads stitched on the outside became his home for the winter.

Always make room for one more in your group.

APPRECIATING DIFFERENCES

Storytelling Tips

🌀 Encourage the listeners to join you in saying the phrases, "the beautiful furry mitten, with tiny, shiny beads stitched on the outside" and "Yes, of course, there's always room for one more."

🌀 Use animal voices to say, "Oh, it is so cold outside. Please, may I come in?" and let the listeners answer, "Yes, of course. There's always room for one more."

🌀 Retell the story and let the listeners use voices that sound like the animals.

🌀 Let the listeners think up new animals for the story. Use animals and birds from your locale. For example, if you live in the Southwest, use coyote, jack rabbit, and roadrunner.

🌀 For younger children, shorten the story by using fewer animals, but always end with the mountain lion or a huge animal, followed by the tiny cricket, a tiny grasshopper, or a tiny ant.

Questions

🌀 How do mittens feel inside? (Provide mittens, if necessary.)

🌀 What surprised you in the story? What was the big surprise at the end?

🌀 Have you ever snuggled into something warm on a cold day? What was it and how did it feel?

MITTEN MATH

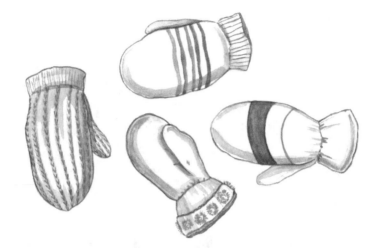

Materials

Several pairs of mittens and gloves

Steps

◉ Collect an assortment of mittens and gloves.

◉ Mix up the mittens and gloves.

◉ Invite the listeners to count them one by one, not in pairs.

◉ Next, have the listeners make pairs.

◉ When the mates are found, count the number of pairs.

◉ Count by two's.

◉ There may be some gloves or mittens without a match. When there is only one mitten, wonder aloud where the lost mitten might be and if there are any animals living inside the lost mitten, wherever it might be.

Adapted from *Story S-t-r-e-t-c-h-e-r-s: Activities to Expand Children's Favorite Books* by Shirley Raines and Robert Canady (1989). Gryphon House: Beltsville, MD.

APPRECIATING DIFFERENCES

MITTEN, MITTEN, WHO HAS THE MITTEN?

Materials

Mitten • music

Steps

◉ Sit in a circle on the floor.

◉ Remember all the animals in "The Lost Mitten With Tiny, Shiny Beads."

◉ Each person chooses an animal from the story.

◉ Explain the game. It is like playing the game of Drop the Handkerchief. The music starts. Each person closes his or her eyes. The child chosen as Little Boy (or Little Girl) walks around behind the animals seated in a circle. When the music stops, Little Boy drops the mitten behind the animal. The person who has the mitten dropped behind him or her picks up the mitten and chases the Little Boy around the circle, trying to tag him before he reaches the empty spot in the circle. Then, the person who now has the mitten follows the same routine.

◉ Continue the game of playing the music, stopping it, dropping the mitten, and chasing around to the empty spot until everyone has had a turn.

ADDITIONAL ANIMALS

Materials

Copies of *The Mitten* by Alvin Tresselt and *The Mitten* by Jan Brett
paper and markers

Steps

◉ After telling "The Lost Mitten With Tiny, Shiny Beads" several
times, read aloud the Tresselt or Brett versions from published
books.

◉ Make a list of all the animals in your told story.

◉ Compile a list of animals in the published books.

◉ Let the children think of some other animals they would like to
have in the story if they were telling their own.

◉ Over the course of a few weeks, let the children tell their versions
of "The Lost Mitten With Tiny, Shiny Beads," using different animals.

APPRECIATING DIFFERENCES

Hearing Music Everywhere

The Four Musicians

FOUR ANIMALS, ALL DISCARDED BY THEIR MAS-
TERS, BECOME A BAND OF MUSICIANS IN THIS
STORY BASED ON A GRIMM'S FAIRY TALE. THEY
SCARE A GROUP OF ROBBERS AWAY FROM A
HOUSE AND DECIDE TO LIVE TOGETHER AND
MAKE MUSIC.

Once there was a donkey who

had worked for many years, day in and day out, carrying heavy sacks of grain for his master. Now that the donkey was older, his master decided to get rid of him. The donkey heard of his master's plan and decided to run away.

Years before, in the city of Bremen, the donkey had heard bands playing music. The donkey said, "I make a very loud noise when I bray. I can be a musician like those in the band." So the donkey set out to become a street musician. As he was walking down the road he saw a dog lying on the ground. He looked very tired and he was panting.

"Why do you look so tired?" asked the donkey.

> "I am not strong enough to go hunting, so my master doesn't want me anymore," said the dog.

Speak in a tired voice.

"Come go with me. I am going to Bremen to be a street musician," said the donkey. The dog thought that was a very good idea. They both walked down the road together, the donkey and the dog.

Much farther down the road they saw a cat sitting by the road. The cat looked very sad. Her sorrowful meowing broke the hearts of the donkey and the dog.

The donkey asked, "Whatever made you so sad, cat?"

Speak in a sad voice.

The cat explained that her teeth were no longer very sharp and she had trouble catching mice. What was she to do?

"Come go with us. We are going to be street musicians.

You can sing and make night music with our band of musicians." The cat was pleased that they thought she could sing, so she joined the band of the donkey and dog. They walked down the road together, the donkey, the dog, and the cat.

The group walked for many miles before they came to a barnyard. On the fence was a rooster, crowing with all his might.

The donkey asked the rooster, "Why are you crowing so loudly?"

Speak in a desperate voice.

The rooster said, "I have just heard the most awful news. Company is coming on Sunday and my master wants to put me in the soup."

"Come go with us. We are going to Bremen to be street musicians. You have a very loud voice. Please join our band of musicians." The rooster was proud of his fine voice, so he flew down from the fence and joined the band. Now there were four musicians who walked down the road together: the donkey, the dog, the cat, and the rooster.

It was a very long way to the city of Bremen, and they needed a place to rest for the night. The rooster flew up in a tree and spied a house nearby. He flew to the house and saw a warm fire in the fireplace. Together the four animals, the donkey, the dog, the cat, and the rooster, decided that the house would be a good place for them to stay for a night.

When they came to the house, the donkey, who was the tallest, looked in the window to see what was inside. The donkey saw a table filled with good things to eat and drink. He noticed bags of gold and silver stacked around the table. He also saw a group of robbers eating the food and enjoying themselves. The four musicians, the donkey, the dog, the cat, and the rooster, devised a plan to scare the robbers away. After the robbers were gone they would eat the delicious food and have a place to stay for the night.

Pretend to eat delicious food.

The donkey stood on his hind legs with his front feet on the window. The dog stood on the donkey's back. The cat climbed onto the dog's back. The rooster flew to the very top and stood on the cat's back. Then they all began singing together. The donkey brayed. The dog barked. The cat meowed. The rooster crowed.

When they sang together, they made so much noise that the windows of the house shattered.

"What a horrible noise! It must be a terrible monster," said the robbers, who were so frightened that they ran away and left all the wonderful food and drink behind for the musicians. The donkey, the dog, the cat, and the rooster ate and ate and ate till they could eat no more. The four musicians liked the house and food so much that they decided to stay for the night. The donkey lay down in the yard. The dog lay down behind the door in the house. The cat curled up by the fire. The rooster flew to the top of the roof. They were all so tired from their long trip that they fell asleep very quickly.

Rub you full stomach with pleasure.

The robbers had been hiding outside in the woods. When they saw the lights go out, they decided to go back to the house and try to find out what had made the horrible noise. One of the robbers went to the house to

Pretend to walk quietly on tiptoe.

see if anything was inside. He went into the house. It was very dark. He saw the green eyes of the cat by the fire and this startled him. But when he struck a match to see better, the cat jumped at him and scratched him. As he ran to the door the dog, who was sleeping by the door, barked and bit him on his leg. In the yard the donkey kicked him and the rooster screamed loudly, "Cock-a-doodle-doo!"

The man was so frightened that he told the other robbers, "There is a horrible monster in the house. It has green eyes that glow in the dark, long arms with sharp nails, big white teeth, strong steel legs, and it makes a terrible screaming sound." When the robbers heard the story about the monster, they all ran away. They never returned to the house again.

The four musicians had found themselves a good home. They had enough silver and gold to buy food and drink to last for the rest of their lives. They decided not to go to Bremen but to make music together in their new home.

They are probably still there today making music: the donkey, the dog, the cat, and the rooster.

By working together you can accomplish more than you can alone.

HEARING MUSIC EVERYWHERE

Storytelling Tips

- Practice using a unique voice for each animal. This will help the listeners follow the story and understand which animal is talking.

- Since an underlying idea in the story is that the animals think they can make music, make the donkey bray, hee-haw; the dog bark, bow-wow; the cat meow; and the rooster, cock-a-doodle-doo. Be sure that voices you use for the animal sounds are not too loud. Young children are sometimes frightened by very loud noises.

- Include all the animals' sounds in sequence and for emphasis repeat the sequence. Observe your audience's response to determine the impact and the number of the repetitions needed.

- Tell the segment of the story where the robber returns to the dark house in a very quiet voice. This variation will make the audience listen more intently to the description of the monster with eyes that glow, sharp white teeth, steel legs, and a screeching voice.

Questions

- Who were the four musicians and what sounds did they make?

- What plan did the musicians develop to scare away the robbers?

- Why did the robber think a "Monster" was in the dark house?

ANIMAL DRAMA

Materials

None needed

Steps

◉ Retell the story or discuss the characters and events.

◉ Invite the listeners to choose a character to play.

◉ Act out the story together. Use your own words and sounds for the animals in the story. In creative dramatics there are no rehearsal or props. Keep the action spontaneous; create the language as the drama takes place.

◉ Dramatize the story again, choosing different parts. Each time the story is dramatized, the events may be different and the language varied.

◉ Encourage the beginning efforts of the listeners. There is no concern for great production, only an opportunity to participate in a creative process.

MAKING MUSIC

Materials

Collection of tapes and/or CDs of different types of musical recordings, including marching band music, folk music, rock music, symphony orchestra, choral groups, and individual instruments such as guitar, piano, or flute.

Steps

- Examine a collection of musical recordings. Look at covers, types, and groups that are included in the collection. Talk about the collection.

- Listen to some of the recordings. Rather than evaluating the recordings, discuss the sounds, songs, instruments, or group. Listen for enjoyment and appreciation of the different kinds of music.

- Select recordings to listen to at different times of the day: music to accompany lunch, music for resting, music for playing, or music for dancing. There is no right or wrong answer, only a personal view and appreciation of the music.

The Sparrow Who Couldn't Sing

A SPARROW THAT CAN'T SING
TRIES TO FIND SOMEONE TO
TEACH HIM,
BUT NOTHING
WORKS. WHEN HE "CROAKS" BY A
POND, FROGS HEAR HIM AND
ASSURE HIM THAT HE CAN SING
BEAUTIFULLY.

Once there was a little Sparrow

who didn't know how to sing. When the other birds sang the Sparrow would try to sing, too. But when he tried to sing he made a horrible sound, "Craawk, craawk, craawk." All the other birds would cover their ears. They couldn't understand how a bird could not sing. The Sparrow was very unhappy because he couldn't sing. He tried and tried and practiced and practiced so he would sound better. All the practice didn't seem to help. He still made a horrible noise, "Craawk, craawk, craawk." So the Sparrow simply stopped trying to sing. He flew and he walked, but he did not sing.

Cover your ears.

One day he saw a Wise Owl in a big hollow tree. His friend the Wise Owl asked the Sparrow why he looked so sad.

"Cheer up," he said, "things can't be all that bad."

The Sparrow said, "Things are pretty bad. I'm a bird and I can't sing. How much worse could it be?"

The Wise Owl said, "All you need is someone to show you how to sing." Together the Wise Owl and the Sparrow went to find someone to show him how to sing. They came to a Cow, who was standing by the fence and "mooing." The Wise Owl told the Cow that the Sparrow needed someone to show him how to sing.

The Cow said, "When I sing all I have to do is go moo, moo, moo." The Sparrow liked the Cow's singing. He tried to sing like the Cow but all that came out was "craawk, craawk, craawk." The Wise Owl and Cow covered their ears. The sounds the Sparrow was making were horrible.

Moo like a cow.

Squeak like a mouse.

The Owl and Sparrow continued down the road looking for someone to show Sparrow how to sing. They heard a tiny mouse singing.

They stopped and asked, "Can you show the Sparrow how to sing?"

"Of course," said the mouse. "When I sing all I have to do is go squeak, squeak, squeak." The Sparrow tried very hard to sing like the mouse. All that came out was "craawk, craawk, craawk." The Wise Owl and Mouse covered their ears. The sounds the Sparrow was making were horrible. It was worse than before.

The Owl and Sparrow continued their search for someone to show Sparrow how to sing. They came to a pond were a Mother Duck was swimming with her baby ducklings.

Quack like a duck.

The Owl told the Mother Duck that the Sparrow was looking for someone to show him how to sing.

The Mother Duck said, "Of course. All we have to do is to go quack, quack, quack." The Mother Duck and her ducklings all quacked together. Again the Sparrow tried to sing like the Ducks. But the only sounds he made were, "craawk, craawk, craawk." The Owl, the Mother Duck, and the Ducklings all covered their ears. The noise was horrible.

Now the Sparrow was getting very discouraged. He said, "It's no use. I am never going to be able to sing. I can't sing."

"Don't give up," said the Wise Owl. "Keep trying. Perhaps you should practice singing some more. Stay here all by yourself and practice your singing."

The Sparrow sat down by the pond. He tried singing very

quietly so as not to make that horrible noise. He sang in his cracking, croaky voice, "craawk, craawk, craawk."

He sang a little louder, "craawk, craawk, craawk." A Big Green Frog jumped up on a lily pad in the pond.

"What a beautiful song you are singing," said the Big Green Frog. "Let's sing together."

The Sparrow was very surprised. He had never met anyone who liked his singing. "All I can do is croak," he answered.

The Big Green Frog replied, "I know and it sounds so beautiful." The Frog and the Sparrow sang together. They sang with their best singing voices, "craawk, craawk, craawk." Soon all the other frogs in the pond came to hear the singing, "craawk, craawk, craawk." All the frogs joined in the song with the Big Green Frog and the Sparrow.

"I can sing! I can sing!" shouted the Sparrow. All the frogs flapped the water and cheered,
"The Sparrow can sing!"

If you keep trying, you will find a place where your talents are appreciated.

143

Storytelling Tips

◉ Experiment with different ways to produce Sparrow's croaking sounds. Find the way that is comfortable for you and replicate it throughout the story.

◉ When the Sparrow is discouraged and practices by the pond, make his first tries barely audible. Increase the volume of each of his following practices. Watch the audience to determine the appropriate maximum level of the sounds for sensitive little ears.

◉ When all the other frogs join Frog and Sparrow, encourage all the listeners to croak together. It may not sound like music, but it will demonstrate how much they can enjoy singing together.

Questions

◉ Why did the Sparrow want to sing?

◉ How did the Wise Owl help the Sparrow learn how to sing?

◉ What were some of the different ways the animals sang in the story?

SINGING SOUNDS

Materials

CD's or tapes of singers, both solo and group performances

Steps

- Play a number of different musical recordings of singers.

- Talk about the singers, sounds, and songs on the recordings.

- Ask the listeners to select recordings they like. Ask what they like about the music.

- Select recordings that you like and explain why these are your favorites.

- Remember that musical taste varies and changes over time.

LIVE MUSIC

Materials

A musician or group of musicians

Steps

 Find a location where musicians will be performing. An informal environment or rehearsal will work best for young listeners. In this setting they can sing or move to the music without restrictions, increasing the enjoyment of the performance.

Take the listeners to the musical performance.

While returning from the musical performance, sing some favorite songs together.

BANG, TAP, RING

Materials

Rhythm instruments or items that will produce a musical sound, including a drum, rhythm sticks, and bells

Steps

🌀 Experiment with the sounds that all the different instruments make.

🌀 Identify the characters in the story (Cow, Mouse, Ducks, and Frog) that tried to show the Sparrow how to sing.

🌀 Together, select an instrument to represent the sound that each animal makes.

🌀 Retell the story with the listeners using the instruments to make musical sounds that accompany the story.

The King's Drum

IN THIS VERSION OF AN ANANSI STORY, THE KING WANTS TO FIND A WAY TO CALL HIS PEOPLE TO IMPORTANT MEETINGS. EVERYONE WORKS TO BUILD A BIG DRUM EXCEPT THE MONKEY. THEY DECIDE THAT THE LAZY MONKEY SHOULD CARRY THE BIG DRUM FROM THE FOREST TO THE KING.

Once there was a King who often called meetings of all of his subjects. The King would send a messenger to the villagers to tell them of his meeting. Many of the villages were far away from the King's home, and it took many weeks for the messages to get to the King's subjects. After they received the message, they would put on their best clothes and walk the long distance to the meeting. It took a long time to get the message and a long time to make the trip. Many weeks would go by before the villagers arrived for the King's meeting.

When all the subjects finally arrived, the King gathered them at his house. He told them his concerns. "When I call a meeting, it is many weeks before we can all be together. What if there was a great danger of an enemy coming? We must get together faster."

Speak in a tone of great importance.

The King's chief advisor was Anansi, the spider. He told the King, "What we need is a huge drum. The kind of drum with a big, loud sound that could be heard for many miles. Everyone would hear the big sound of the drum and come quickly."

Make the sounds of a drum.

The King and all the animals liked Anansi's idea: Build a huge drum. All the animals formed teams to build the drum. One team went into the forest to find a tree. Another team trimmed and shaped the tree for the drum. Another group hollowed the tree out to help create the deep sound of the drum. A group of carvers decorated the drum so it would be beautiful.

Pretend to be sleeping.

Everyone except Monkey worked on the drum. Monkey just slept in the shade. Anansi saw that Monkey was not working. While all the other animals were working on the drum, Monkey was resting.

Anansi said, "The drum is ready for the King."

There was only one problem: Who would carry the drum? The drum was large and heavy. It was a very long way from the forest to the King's house. No one wanted to carry the large and heavy drum.

Lion said, "Antelope can carry the drum."

Antelope said, "Elephant can carry the drum." Each animal thought another animal should carry the drum.

Anansi said, "No one wants to carry the heavy drum all the way to the King's home. I think that the laziest person should carry the drum."

The King agreed, "That is how it should be done."

The animals thought, "Who is the laziest?" One by one each of the animals looked at Monkey. Monkey saw that everyone was looking at him. He walked to the middle of the animals and announced, "I will not carry this heavy drum."

Everyone laughed, "No one called your name, Monkey. We were simply asked to decide who was the laziest. You have told us you are the laziest when you spoke."

The animals all agreed, "Monkey is the laziest of all."

And so it was that Monkey carried the large and heavy drum from the forest to the King's house.

Everyone needs to do their share of the work.

Storytelling Tips

◉ Before telling this story talk about the character Anansi, the spider. Explain that sometimes he is clever and full of mischief, and sometimes he does silly things. In most of the stories he uses his wits to outsmart others or to accomplish his goal.

◉ Use a drum to enrich the telling of the story, either as an introduction to the story or to call the celebration in the story.

Questions

◉ What was the problem the King wanted to solve?

◉ How did different animals work on the drum? What were their jobs?

◉ How did the monkey get the job of carrying the drum from the forest to the King's house?

DRUM ECHOES

Materials

Drums or pots

Steps

◉ Play a short pattern on the drum or pot.

◉ Let the listeners echo the pattern on another drum or pot.

◉ Repeat another pattern, and let the listeners echo the same pattern.

◉ Let one listener create a short pattern, and you echo the pattern.

◉ Continue with echo responses until the children tire of the activity.

URGENT MESSAGES

Materials

An empty coffee can
with a plastic lid • a
drum • or a pot

Steps

◉ Discuss what kind
of messages could
be sent on the
drum, including
come to the feast,
danger, fish are bit-
ing, village meeting.

◉ Encourage the lis-
teners to create a pattern that will send a specific message.

◉ How are the messages different?

◉ Use the drum to send messages during the day including rest
time, dinner is ready, time to come inside.

The Nightingale

A PLAIN NIGHTINGALE WITH A BEAUTI-
FUL SONG IS REPLACED BY A MECHANI-
CAL BEJEWELED NIGHTINGALE IN THIS
ADAPTATION OF A HANS CHRISTIAN
ANDERSON TALE, BUT SHE RETURNS
LATER TO SING FOR THE SICK EMPEROR.

Once upon a time, in a royal empire, there lived a gracious Emperor. He had a magnificent palace, with beautiful gardens that stretched as far as the eye could see. Hundreds of gardeners tended the lovely flowers, the blossoming trees, and glassy reflecting pools. The gardens were so vast that they stretched down through three meadows to the sea.

Point to a place far in the distance.

There by the shore, a poor fisherman kept his boat. One of the fisherman's great pleasures was to listen to the beautiful melodious song of the nightingale. The nightingale lived in the tall tree in the third meadow.

Each night as the poor fisherman listened, the nightingale's song brought him peace and rest so that the next day he was able to return again to his hard work.

Many people from far and wide came to the Emperor's royal estate to view the beautiful gardens and stay in the magnificent palaces. The Emperor's guests always complimented the Emperor and told him that his palace and gardens were the most beautiful in the world.

When the guests returned to their homes, they wrote letters to the Emperor and thanked him for his hospitality. One guest wrote, "The most beautiful part of your empire is the song of the nightingale."

The Emperor was surprised. He had not ever heard the song of the nightingale. The meadow where the nightingale lived was far from the palace. As a matter of fact, he did not even know there was a bird called a nightingale. The Emperor summoned his royal guards and commanded them to find this bird that sang the beautiful song. Since the guards never ventured past the palace doors, they had not heard the beautiful song of the nightingale. Just like the Emperor, they did not even know there was a bird called a nightingale. The royal guards had no idea where to start looking for the nightingale.

The poor maid who scrubbed the palace floors overheard the royal guards discussing the Emperor's command that they find this bird called a nightingale. The poor maid told the royal guards that she had heard the nightingale's song. She said, "The nightingale's song is so sweet. Each night when I go to my little home in the meadow I hear it and I am comforted. The beautiful melodious song brings me peace and rest, so that I can return the next day to my hard work."

Say this with a peaceful expression on your face.

The royal guards commanded the poor maid to lead them to the place where the nightingale lived. The royal guards followed the poor maid out of the palace, down through the many gardens, and out to the first meadow. In the first meadow, they heard the cow moo. They bowed down to the ground and said, "We have found the beautiful song of the nightingale." The poor maid laughed and said that it was only the farmer's cows, not the nightingale.

Moo like a cow.

Farther along the road, which ran through the second meadow, the royal guards heard another sound that they had never heard before. There were frogs croaking in the farmer's pond. When they heard this new sound, the royal guards bowed down to the ground and said, "We have found the beautiful song of the nightingale." The poor maid laughed and said that it was only the croaking frogs who live at the edge of the farmer's pond, not the nightingale.

Croak like a frog.

157

Near dusk the poor maid and the royal guards came to the third meadow, where the tall tree stood. The poor maid asked everyone to be very quiet and still. They did, which was not easy for royal guards, who were also royal chatterboxes. When it was still and quiet, the nightingale began to sing the most beautiful melodious song the royal guards had ever heard.

The royal guards bowed down to the ground and exclaimed, "At last, we have found the royal nightingale." They begged the nightingale to hop down from the tree. The nightingale did what was requested and hopped onto the shoulder of the poor maid.

The royal guards were surprised to see the nightingale was just a plain drab gray bird with shabby wings. They had expected a beautiful bird of many colors, with wings as smooth as silk.

The poor maid asked, "Nightingale, will you come back to the palace and sing for the Emperor?" The nightingale explained that she had never sung in a palace. She sang her best in the cool air in an open space, but she would try. Nightingale did not want to disappoint the poor maid, who appreciated her song. So, the plain gray nightingale accompanied the royal guards and the poor maid back through the three meadows to the Emperor's palace.

Pretend to stroke long, smooth silk robes.

Back at the palace, the royal guards, the poor maid, and the nightingale greeted the great Emperor, who was dressed in his most beautiful silk robes. He sat upon his royal throne, which sparkled with jewels. Seeing the small gray bird, the Emperor wondered how one so plain could sing beautifully.

Yet, when the nightingale sang her beautiful melodious song, the Emperor was so touched that big tears flowed from his eyes and flowed down his great beard. He was overcome with joy. He had never heard a song so sweet.

The nightingale was pleased, knowing that her song made the Emperor so happy. The Emperor offered the nightingale his golden slipper as a nest and a golden perch as a place to sit and sing. The nightingale replied, "Thank you, great Emperor."

The nightingale stayed on in the palace to sing for the Emperor and the poor maid. Each night when the nightingale sang, the poor maid was comforted. The *Sigh happily.* beautiful melodious song brought her peace and rest so that she could return the next day to her hard work.

Weeks later, a special package arrived from one of the guests who had visited in the Emperor's palace. Inside the package was a present for the Emperor. It was a mechanical bird that could sing a beautiful song. The mechanical bird was of many colors, encrusted with diamonds, rubies, emeralds, and sapphires. In the package there was a card. The card said, "Wind up the mechanical bird and listen to it sing."

When the royal guards wound up the beautiful bird, *Gasp in* encrusted with jewels, it bobbed up and down and *surprise.* began to sing. Everyone praised the wind-up bird, mar-

Sigh happily.

veled at the mechanical song, and admired the beautiful jewels. The Emperor asked the real nightingale to sing a duet with the wind-up bird. Nightingale tried, but their songs did not go together.

The royal guards and the Emperor enjoyed hearing the mechanical bird sing. They wound up the bird again and again and played the song over and over. While they were playing the wind-up bird, the nightingale flew through the window, down the long expanse of the garden, through the three meadows, and into the top of the tall tree. That night, the nightingale sang her song for the poor fisherman. He had missed the song. He thanked the nightingale for her beautiful, melodious song. The song comforted him. It brought him peace and rest so that he could return the next day to his hard work.

The Emperor missed the real nightingale's song at night, but the wind-up bird encrusted with jewels was a beautiful sight and he could hear the song whenever he wanted by simply winding up the bird.

Then one day, the wind-up mechanical bird bobbed up and bobbed down, but no song came out. It whirred and clicked, clacked and stopped. It stood still and silent. The Emperor was upset. He called the royal "fix-it" man to fix the bird. He was able to fix the bird, but he told the Emperor not to play it so often. So, once a day at bedtime, the Emperor wound the mechanical nightingale and listened to the song. But the song was never the same as when it was new, and it only reminded the Emperor of the real nightingale, whose song was so beautiful and melodious.

Months later, the Emperor became very sick. He wished for music to give him rest. He saw the mechanical nightingale beside his bed. He wound it up, but the song was so unpleasant that it did not comfort him.

The poor maid, cleaning in the Emperor's room, overheard him say that he needed music to give him rest. She left the palace and walked to the tall tree in the third meadow. The poor maid told the nightingale that the Emperor was very ill. He had one wish—music to give him rest. The nightingale returned to the palace with the poor maid and sang for the great Emperor, who was gravely ill.

Each night for a month, the nightingale sang to the Emperor. The nightingale's beautiful melodious song comforted the great Emperor and brought him peace **Sigh happily.** and rest so that he could get well.

The great Emperor was grateful to the little gray nightingale and felt guilty for his attraction to the mechanical bird encrusted with jewels. The Emperor said, "I shall break the mechanical bird encrusted with jewels into a thousand pieces."

But the nightingale said, "No, great Emperor, the mechanical bird encrusted with jewels is still a beautiful thing, it simply cannot sing."

The great Emperor asked the nightingale to live in the palace and to sing for him each night, but the nightingale replied, "No, great Emperor, but I will fly about your kingdom. Once a month I will return to you to sing a song of what is happening in your empire. I will sing about the rich and the poor, the happy and the sad, the sick and the well, so that you might know what is happening outside your palace walls. I will be the little bird that sits on your shoulder and tells you everything."

"Everything and anything, anything and everything?" asked the great Emperor. "Everything and anything," sang the nightingale. The nightingale's beautiful, melodious song comforted the great Emperor and brought him peace and rest so that he could return to ruling.

Sigh happily.

And, to this day, the old Emperor is the wisest Emperor of all. How do I know? A little gray bird from the third meadow told me so.

Appreciate people for their unique abilities, regardless of appearances.

Storytelling Tips

- Make the story your own. Do not worry if your descriptions and phrasing are different. Read the story several times and write your own outline (or refer to the story card on page 194). Some people remember stories by key phrases, some by settings, and some by characters.

- Encourage the listeners to join you in saying the repeated phrases, "The beautiful, melodious song of the nightingale brought peace and rest."

- Add a xylophone to the telling of the story. Each time the real nightingale's song is sung, run the mallet across the bars from the lowest to the highest with a light stoke.

- Use hand motions to illustrate winding up the mechanical bird and the royal "fix-it" man trying to fix the bird.

- Bow down to the ground when telling about the royal guards hearing the sounds of the cow, the frog, and finally the nightingale.

Questions

- Do you like playing with a wind-up toy car or riding in a small car at an amusement park?

- Would you like to see a stuffed toy bird or a real bird? Why?

- What is the difference between a walk in the woods and a video of a walk in the woods?

REAL VERSUS MECHANICAL

Materials

Wind-up or stuffed toy animal • real animal

Steps

◉ Enjoy playing with the cat or dog.

◉ Wind-up the toy animal (or put out the stuffed animal).

◉ Play with the wind-up animal and ignore the real pet.

◉ Talk about how it is different to play with the real animal as compared to playing with the mechanical wind-up toy (or the stuffed animal).

REAL OR PRETEND?

Materials

Encyclopedia (book or CD) or book about birds, paper, marker

Steps

 Ask the listeners if they have ever seen a nightingale or heard a nightingale sing.

 Wonder aloud if the nightingale is a real bird or a pretend bird.

 Print the word "nightingale" on a sheet of paper.

 With the listeners, look up the word "nightingale" in a source, such as a book about birds or an encyclopedia.

 Read aloud what the book or encyclopedia says about the nightingale. Let the listeners decide if the nightingale is a real bird or a bird in a story.

PLEASE TELL IT AGAIN

Materials

Paper • marker

Steps

◉ Draw the shape of a bird on a sheet of paper or write the word "nightingale" on a sheet of paper and give it to a child.

◉ Retell the story and invite the listener to hold up the sheet of paper each time you say the word "nightingale." If you are telling the story to several listeners, give them other sheets of paper with the name or outline of different characters in the story on each.

Story Cards

TEENY TINY

CHARACTERS: TEENY TINY WOMAN, TEENY TINY DOG, VOICE

◉ Teeny tiny woman lives in a teeny tiny house.

◉ One night she goes for a teeny tiny walk.

◉ She walks through a graveyard and finds a bone.

◉ She carries it home for her teeny tiny dog.

◉ She puts the bone in a teeny tiny cupboard.

◉ She climbs into her teeny tiny bed.

◉ Faraway teeny tiny voice calls, "Give me my bone!"

◉ Frightened, she pulls up teeny tiny covers.

◉ She hears teeny tiny front door open.

◉ Closer, louder voice says, "Give me my bone!"

◉ She slides further under the teeny tiny covers.

◉ She hears creaks on teeny tiny stairs.

◉ She hears a voice say, "Give me my bone!"

◉ Teeny tiny woman sits up.

◉ She answers in a not so teeny tiny voice,

◉ "Take it!"

THE KNEE-HIGH MAN

CHARACTERS: KNEE-HIGH MAN, MR. HORSE,
MR. BULL, MR. HOOT OWL

- Knee-High Man was no taller than your knees.

- He wanted to be bigger, taller, and stronger.

- He asked Mr. Horse how he could do this.

- Mr. Horse said to eat bushels of corn and run.

- Knee-High Man did, but got a stomach and leg ache.

- Then he asked Mr. Bull the same question.

- Mr. Bull said to eat acres of grass and bellow.

- Knee-High Man did, but got a throat ache, too.

- He asked Mr. Hoot Owl the same question.

- Mr. Hoot Owl asked why he wanted to change.

- Knee-High Man said so no one picked on him.

- Mr. Hoot Owl asked if anyone had picked on him.

- Knee-High Man said no, but he wanted to see farther.

- Mr. Hoot Owl told him to climb a tree to see farther.

- Knee-High Man didn't need to change himself.

- He just needed to use his brain.

THE STORY OF THE UGLY DUCKLING

CHARACTERS: MOTHER DUCK, BABY DUCKS, UGLY DUCKLING,
OTHER DUCKS, OLD WOMAN, FARMER, WIFE, CHILDREN, SWANS

- A mother duck sat on her eggs in the forest.

- The eggs began to hatch into lovely ducklings.

- The biggest egg hatched into an ugly duckling.

- Mother duck led her babies to the water.

- The other ducks made fun of the ugly duckling.

- He ran away and hid in the marsh.

- The wild ducks in the marsh made fun of him.

- He found a new home with an old woman.

- Her cottage was gloomy so he returned to the lake.

- The ugly duckling became frozen in the cold lake.

- A farmer freed him and took him home.

- The farmer's wife and children made fun of him.

- The ugly duckling ran away to the marsh.

- When spring came he saw some beautiful swans.

- Then he saw his own reflection in the water.

- He was amazed to see that he was a beautiful swan.

- Children said he was the prettiest swan of all.

TELL IT AGAIN!

THREE BILLY GOATS GRUFF

CHARACTERS: LITTLE BILLY GOAT GRUFF, MIDDLE-SIZED BILLY GOAT GRUFF, GREAT BIG BILLY GOAT GRUFF, OLD TROLL

- Little Billy Goat Gruff, Middle-Sized Billy Goat Gruff, and Great Big Billy Goat Gruff lived on a hillside.

- The older Billy Goats warned Little Billy Goat not to cross the bridge because a mean old troll lived under it.

- Little Billy Goat wanted to eat the grass on the other side.

- Trip-trap, trip-trap, he came trip-trapping across the bridge.

- "Who is that trip-trapping across my bridge?" asked the troll.

- The troll threatened to eat him up, but Little Billy Goat told him to wait for Middle-Sized Billy Goat instead.

- The troll let him pass and waited for his brother.

- Trip-trap, trip-trap, Middle-Sized Billy Goat came trip-trapping across the bridge.

- "Who is that trip-trapping across my bridge?" asked the troll.

- The troll threatened to eat him up, but Middle-Sized Billy Goat told him to wait for Great Big Billy Goat instead.

- The troll let him pass and waited for his brother.

- Trip-trap, trip-trap, Great Big Billy Goat came trip-trapping across the bridge.

◉ "Who is that trip-trapping across my bridge?" asked the troll.

◉ The troll threatened to eat him up.

◉ Great Big Billy Goat said, "See how big and tough I am."

◉ Then he butted the troll off the bridge, and the troll ran away.

◉ The Billy Goats Gruff now cross the bridge every day.

THE TURTLE AND THE RABBIT

CHARACTERS: RABBIT, FRIENDS, TURTLE, FOX, CROWDS

- A rabbit was very proud that he could run fast.
- He met a turtle moving slowly down the road.
- He made fun of the turtle for being so slow.
- The turtle claimed to be quicker than the rabbit.
- The rabbit challenged the turtle to a race.
- The race began and the rabbit speedily took off.
- Soon the rabbit noticed the turtle was far behind.
- He decided to take a rest in the warm sun.
- The turtle kept on moving, slow and steady.
- The turtle passed the sleeping rabbit.
- The rabbit woke up and got back on the road.
- Soon he realized that the turtle was ahead of him.
- The turtle crossed the finish line first.

NAIL SOUP

⊚ A hungry tramp knocked on the door of a cottage.

⊚ An old woman let him in but said there was no food.

⊚ He told her how he could make a delicious soup by boiling a nail in a pot of water.

⊚ The curious woman wanted to taste the nail soup.

⊚ The tramp dropped a nail in a half-full pot of water and put it on the stove.

⊚ The tramp said: "Nail soup, nail soup, delicious nail soup. Madam, when I cooked the soup last night, all it needed was some **salt and pepper**. I don't suppose you have a **bit of salt and some pepper**, do you? The batch of soup I made last night just needed some **salt and pepper** to make it just right."

⊚ The old woman said: "**Salt and pepper**? I might just have some **salt and pepper** left in this empty cupboard."

⊚ The tramp added the **salt and pepper** to the bubbling water with the nail.

> Repeat above (starting with "The tramp said..."), substituting: **half an onion, a few carrots, a few potatoes, a small head of cabbage** in place of **salt and pepper.**

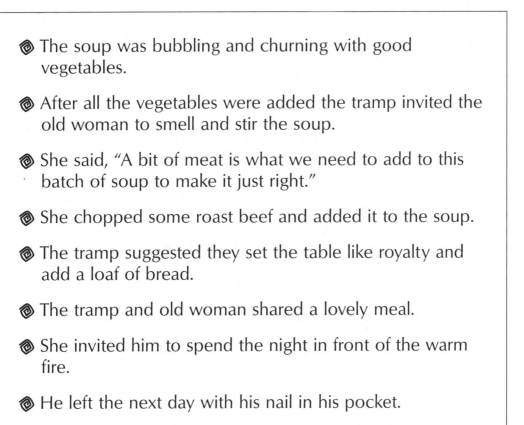

- The soup was bubbling and churning with good vegetables.

- After all the vegetables were added the tramp invited the old woman to smell and stir the soup.

- She said, "A bit of meat is what we need to add to this batch of soup to make it just right."

- She chopped some roast beef and added it to the soup.

- The tramp suggested they set the table like royalty and add a loaf of bread.

- The tramp and old woman shared a lovely meal.

- She invited him to spend the night in front of the warm fire.

- He left the next day with his nail in his pocket.

JOHNNY-CAKE

◉ A little old woman made a Johnny-Cake for lunch.

◉ She asked her little boy to watch the oven.

◉ He forgot and out rolled the Johnny-Cake.

◉ The boy yelled, "Stop, stop, stop, Johnny-Cake!"

◉ His parents heard the yelling and joined the chase. They were soon out of breath and sat down on the side of the road.

◉ Johnny-Cake rolled on past two well diggers who yelled, "Johnny-Cake, where are you going so fast?"

◉ Johnny-Cake said, "I ran faster than the little boy, the little old man and the little old woman, and I can run faster than you too-oo-o!"

◉ The well diggers said, "Well, we are faster than they are."

◉ They started to chase Johnny-Cake, but were soon of breath and sat down on the side of the road.

◉ Johnny-Cake rolled on until he passed two ditch diggers who yelled, "Johnny-Cake, where are you going so fast?"

◉ Johnny-Cake said, "I ran faster than..." (list characters)

◉ The ditch diggers said, "Well, we are faster than they are."

◉ They started to chase Johnny-Cake, but were soon of breath and sat down on the side of the road.

- Johnny-Cake rolled on until he passed Bear who growled,"Johnny-Cake, where are you going so fast?"

- Johnny-Cake said, "I ran faster than..." (list characters)

- Bear said, "Well, I am faster than they are."

- Bear started to chase Johnny-Cake, but was soon of breath and sat down on the side of the road.

- Johnny-Cake rolled on until he passed Wolf who howled, "Johnny-Cake, where are you going so fast?"

- Johnny-Cake said, "I ran faster than..." (list characters)

- Wolf said, "Well, I am faster than they are."

- Wolf started to chase Johnny-Cake, but was soon of breath and sat down on the side of the road.

- Johnny-Cake rolled on until he passed Fox who said, "Johnny-Cake, where are you going so fast?"

- Johnny-Cake said, "I ran faster than..." (list characters)

- Fox said, "What did you say? Come closer, I can't hear you."

- Johnny-Cake moved closer and repeated himself.

- Fox said, "Come closer, Johnny Cake, I can't hear you."

- Johnny-Cake moved even closer and repeated himself.

- Fox said, "You can, can you?" and quickly opened his mouth wide and snapped Johnny-Cake between his sharp teeth.

- Fox rolled his foxy eyes and licked his lips.

THE FLYING CONTEST

OR HOW KUNIBRE BECAME KING OF THE BIRDS

CHARACTERS: BIRDS, LION, FALCON, KUNIBRE, NIGHTINGALE

- The Birds wanted a king to rule over the skies.
- They called a meeting of all the birds.
- Lion asked how they wanted to settle the question.
- Falcon knew that he could fly the highest.
- He wanted to suggest that the highest flyer be king.
- Kunibre knew that he was the smallest bird, but smart.
- He wanted to suggest that the smartest bird be king.
- Nightingale knew that he was the best singer.
- But he wanted to find a fair way to settle the contest.
- He said the bird who flies the highest should be king.
- Falcon thought for sure that he would win.
- He didn't notice Kunibre fly onto his back.
- Falcon soared higher and higher into the air.
- When he landed the birds said Falcon should be king.
- Then they noticed that Kunibre was on top of him.
- They made Kunibre king of the birds instead.

TELL IT AGAIN!

THE GREAT GAME IN THE SKY

CHARACTERS: ANIMALS WITH FUR (BEAR, DEER, WOLF, RACCOON, OTTER, BEAVER, RABBIT, AND SQUIRREL); ANIMALS WITH FEATHERS (EAGLE, HAWK, DUCK, STORK, GULL, CROW, BLUE JAY, AND SPARROW); AND BAT

- Long ago, the animals of the woods had a great argument and decided to settle it with a game of lacrosse.

- Animals with fur took the north end of the field, and animals with feathers took the south end of the field.

- A tiny, mysterious creature asked to play, but the animals said no because he had neither fur nor feathers.

- "No one who wants to play should be left out," said Otter, so the tiny creature joined the animals-with-fur side.

- The ball was tossed and Deer grabbed it and ran.

- Stork flew down and got the ball from Deer.

- Wolf got the ball back and tossed it to Beaver.

- Hawk flew down and stole the ball from Beaver.

- The birds kept the ball in the sky until sunset.

- Suddenly the tiny creature flew up, seized the ball, and flew across the southern goal line with it.

- The animals with fur shouted, "We won, we won!"

- The tiny, mysterious creature said his name was Bat.

- From that day on, Bat's reward was to sleep all day and catch all the tasty insects he wanted at night.

BIG CITY MOUSE, SMALL TOWN MOUSE

CHARACTERS: BIG CITY MOUSE, SMALL TOWN MOUSE,
NEIGHBORS, WISE OLD MOUSE

◉ Big City Mouse lived in a penthouse in the city.

◉ Big City Mouse was a very lonely mouse.

◉ Big City Mouse loved hard cheese wrapped in foil.

◉ He hated the screeching traffic and noise of the city.

◉ One day the Doorman brought Big City Mouse a letter.

◉ It said, "Come to Small Town for a Family Reunion. All
your cousins from far and wide will be there for a picnic
in the meadow."

◉ Small Town Mouse had a nice back porch on a meadow.

◉ All his neighbors liked to sit there and watch the sunset.

◉ Small Town Mouse did not like their gossip and chatter.

◉ He did not like cleaning up after they went home.

◉ He longed for fancy hard cheese instead of cottage
cheese.

◉ One evening, a swooping owl scared everyone away.

◉ Someone dropped a letter that said: "Come to Small
Town for a Family Reunion. All your cousins from far
and wide will be there for a picnic in the meadow."

- Small Town Mouse remembered his cousin Big City Mouse.

- He wanted to ask him about life in the city.

- He decided to go to the reunion in the meadow.

- The two mouse cousins shared a table and talked.

- Big City Mouse talked about his life in the big city.

- Small Town Mouse talked about his life in a small town.

- Each mouse thought the other mouse had a better life.

- Wise Old Mouse said, "If you don't like your life, then change it."

- They decided to swap places and try each other's homes.

- Small Town Mouse loved the big, exciting, noisy city.

- Big City Mouse loved a back porch filled with neighbors.

- Every year at the family reunion they would nibble cheese in little foil packages and talk about how lucky they were to live in new places.

"COULD BE WORSE!"

CHARACTERS: GRANDPA, MARY ANN, AND LOUIE

◉ At Grandpa's house things were always the same.

◉ No matter what happened, he would say, "Could be worse."

◉ One day Mary Ann said, "How Come Grandpa never says anything interesting?"

◉ Louie said, "I guess it's because nothing interesting happens to him."

◉ Grandpa overheard the children talking.

◉ The next morning, he said something different.

◉ He said, "Guess what? Last night...

...a bird pulled me out of bed

...an abominable snowman threw a snowball at me

...got stuck inside and rolled down the mountain

...snowball melted in the desert

...got squished by giant something-or-other

...blob of marmalade chased me

...crashed into something tall like an ostrich

...got kicked into the storm clouds

...almost hit by lightning

...landed in an ocean

...sank down a mile to the bottom

...enormous goldfish coming at me

...hid under a cup with air in it

...crawled out and started to walk

...got stuck in grip of gigantic lobster

...didn't know what to do

...squid squirted black ink on lobster

...escaped and hitched ride on sea turtle

...rode a piece of toast to shore

...found a newspaper

...folded it into an airplane

...flew across the sea and back to bed.

◉ Now what do you think of that?" he asked.

◉ "Could be worse!" said the children.

MONKEY'S AND RABBIT'S BAD HABITS

CHARACTERS: MONKEY AND RABBIT

◉ Monkey and Rabbit liked to talk to each other.

◉ But each one had a distracting problem.

◉ Monkey scratched himself while he talked.

◉ Rabbit sniffed and twitched and flopped.

◉ Monkey asked Rabbit to stop his bad habits.

◉ Rabbit complained about Monkey's scratching.

◉ They decided to have a contest to break bad habits.

◉ Monkey agreed to go all day without scratching.

◉ Rabbit agreed to stop sniffing and twitching.

◉ Sitting still was very hard for both of them.

◉ They decided to pass the time by telling stories.

◉ Rabbit told a story about a lion in the grass.

◉ As he talked he sniffed and twitched and flopped.

◉ Monkey told how children threw coconuts at him.

◉ As he talked he scratched his head, chin, and arm.

◉ Rabbit and Monkey both began to laugh.

◉ They agreed they couldn't break their bad habits.

THE WOMAN WHO WANTED MORE NOISE

CHARACTERS: WOMAN, COUSIN, NEIGHBOR, COW, DOG, CAT, DUCKS,
HENS, ROOSTER, LITTLE CHICKS, PIG, CHILDREN

◉ Once there was a woman who lived in the city.

◉ She loved all the noise and sounds of the city.

◉ Her cousin offered her a home in the country.

◉ The city woman thought the farm would be nice.

◉ She liked the land, the orchard, the barn and garden.

◉ But she couldn't sleep at night because it was too quiet.

◉ She asked her neighbor how to make the farm noisier.

◉ Her neighbor told her to buy animals that made noises.

◉ So the woman bought a cow and put it in the barn.

◉ The cow made a fine noise (moo), but it was not
enough.

◉ She bought a dog and fed him well.

◉ The dog made a fine noise (bark), but it was not enough.

◉ She bought a cat and put her in the house.

◉ The cat made a fine noise (meow), but it was not
enough.

◉ She bought some ducks and put them in the pond.

- The ducks made a fine noise (quack), but it was not enough.

- She bought hens, a rooster, and little chicks.

- They made a fine noise (crow), but it was not enough.

- She bought a pig to keep on her farm.

- He made a fine noise (oink), but it was not enough.

- She bought an old broken-down car with a loud horn.

- It made a fine noise (honk), but it was not enough.

- The woman still couldn't sleep at night; it was too quiet.

- The woman brought some children to visit her farm.

- They were very loud and made a fine noise.

- Now the animals would make their sounds, the woman would honk her horn, and the children would play.

- At last the woman felt there was enough noise.

- She could sleep at night with all the beautiful sounds.

THE LOST MITTEN WITH TINY, SHINY BEADS

CHARACTERS: GRANDMOTHER, GRANDSON, FIELD MOUSE, FROG, OWL, RABBIT, FOX, MOUNTAIN LION, CRICKET

◉ A grandmother and her grandson lived by the woods.

◉ One day she sent him to get some kindling wood.

◉ He wore his beautiful furry mittens with tiny, shiny beads that his grandmother had knit him.

◉ The boy pulled his sled deep into the forest to find wood.

◉ He lost one of his beautiful mittens with tiny, shiny beads.

◉ He searched but couldn't find it and went home.

◉ Meanwhile, the beautiful furry mitten with tiny, shiny beads lay in the snow.

◉ Field Mouse was very cold and wiggled inside it.

* ◉ Just as he was settling down, he heard someone say, "It is so cold outside. Please, may I come in?"

◉ "Who is that outside in the cold?" asked Field Mouse.

◉ "It is I, Frog, and I am so cold."

◉ "Yes, of course, there is always room for one more."

◉ So Frog hopped inside the beautiful furry mitten with tiny, shiny beads stitched on the outside.

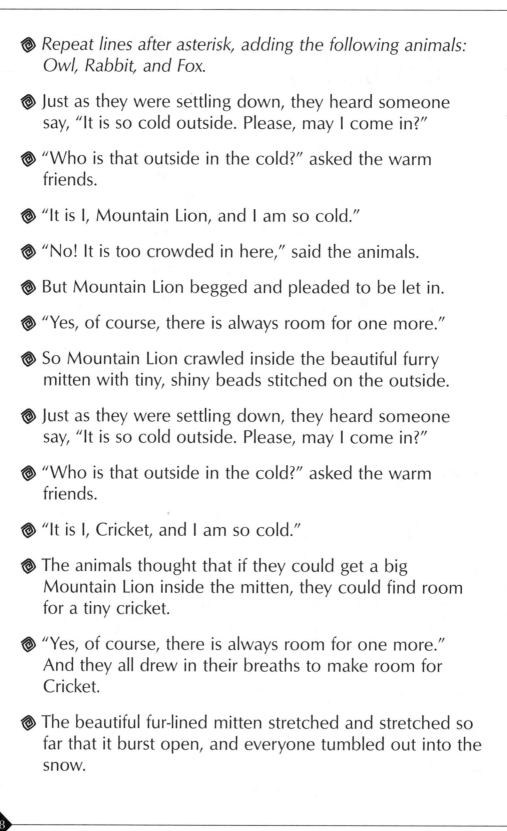

◉ *Repeat lines after asterisk, adding the following animals: Owl, Rabbit, and Fox.*

◉ Just as they were settling down, they heard someone say, "It is so cold outside. Please, may I come in?"

◉ "Who is that outside in the cold?" asked the warm friends.

◉ "It is I, Mountain Lion, and I am so cold."

◉ "No! It is too crowded in here," said the animals.

◉ But Mountain Lion begged and pleaded to be let in.

◉ "Yes, of course, there is always room for one more."

◉ So Mountain Lion crawled inside the beautiful furry mitten with tiny, shiny beads stitched on the outside.

◉ Just as they were settling down, they heard someone say, "It is so cold outside. Please, may I come in?"

◉ "Who is that outside in the cold?" asked the warm friends.

◉ "It is I, Cricket, and I am so cold."

◉ The animals thought that if they could get a big Mountain Lion inside the mitten, they could find room for a tiny cricket.

◉ "Yes, of course, there is always room for one more." And they all drew in their breaths to make room for Cricket.

◉ The beautiful fur-lined mitten stretched and stretched so far that it burst open, and everyone tumbled out into the snow.

◉ All but Cricket ran back to their forest homes.

◉ Cricket found a piece of the mitten with one tiny, shiny bead left on the outside and made it his home.

◉ That spring, the little boy found the scrap of mitten with the cricket inside.

◉ Cricket hopped on his shoulder and told him the whole story.

THE FOUR MUSICIANS

CHARACTERS: DONKEY, DOG, CAT, ROOSTER, ROBBERS

- A donkey learned that his master planned to get rid of him.

- The donkey could make a very loud noise when he brayed.

- He decided to go to Bremen and become a street musician.

- On the way to Bremen, he saw a dog lying on the ground.

- The dog said his master didn't want him anymore.

- "Come go with me," said the donkey. "I am going to Bremen to be a street musician."

- The dog agreed and they walked down the road together, the donkey and the dog.

- They saw a sad looking cat sitting by the road.

- She said her teeth were no longer sharp and she had trouble catching mice.

- "Come go with us," said the donkey. "We are going to Bremen to be street musicians."

- The cat agreed and they all walked down the road together, the donkey, the dog, and the cat.

- They came to a barnyard where a rooster was crowing.

- He had just learned he was going to be put in the soup.

- "Come go with us," said the donkey. "We am going to Bremen to be street musicians."

- The rooster agreed, and they all walked down the road together, the donkey, the dog, the cat, and the rooster.

- They came across a house and decided to spend the night.

- The donkey looked through the window and saw a group of robbers, lots of food, and bags of silver and gold.

- The four musicians made loud noises and frightened the robbers away.

- They settled down to sleep by the warm fire.

- During the night one robber slipped back into the house.

- The cat jumped and scratched him. The dog barked and bit him, the donkey kicked him, and the rooster screamed.

- The robber thought a monster was in the house and never came back.

- The four musicians had a good home with enough silver and gold to last for the rest of their lives.

- They are probably still there, making music together.

THE SPARROW WHO COULDN'T SING

CHARACTERS: SPARROW, WISE OWL, COW, MOUSE,
MOTHER DUCK, GREEN FROG

- A little sparrow did not know how to sing.

- When he tried, he made a horrible sound.

- He told the Wise Owl about his problem.

- They asked Cow to teach Sparrow to sing.

- Cow said to just go moo, moo, moo.

- Sparrow sang, "craawk, craawk, craawk."

- They asked a tiny mouse how to sing.

- He said to just go squeak, squeak, squeak.

- Sparrow tried but still made a horrible sound.

- They asked a Mother Duck how to sing.

- She said to just go quack, quack quack.

- But still Sparrow sang, "craawk, craawk, craawk."

- Wise Owl urged Sparrow not to give up.

- A Green Frog heard him practicing.

- He loved Sparrow's beautiful singing.

- Together they sang, "craawk, craawk, craawk."

TELL IT AGAIN!

THE KING'S DRUM

CHARACTERS: KING, MESSENGER, VILLAGERS, ANANSI, MONKEY

- The King called a meeting of his subjects.
- He sent a messenger to tell the villagers.
- It took many weeks to gather everyone.
- The King wanted a faster way to communicate.
- Anansi, the spider, suggested a huge drum.
- A drum could be heard for many miles.
- The animals organized into work squads.
- They all worked hard to make a drum.
- All except Monkey, who slept instead.
- The King asked the animals to carry the drum.
- It was very heavy and no one wanted to.
- They decided the laziest person should do it.
- They all looked at Monkey but he refused.
- The animals agreed, Monkey was the laziest.
- He had to carry the heavy drum to the King.

THE NIGHTINGALE

CHARACTERS: EMPEROR, NIGHTINGALE, FISHERMAN, GUESTS, GUARDS, MAID, MECHANICAL BIRD

- A gracious Emperor had a magnificent palace.

- A nightingale lived in one of his gardens.

- Her beautiful song pleased many guests.

- The Emperor had his guards find the bird.

- A poor maid took the guards to the nightingale.

- The Emperor loved her beautiful singing.

- Later he received a mechanical bird as a gift.

- The jeweled wind-up bird bobbed and sang.

- The Emperor liked the mechanical bird.

- The real nightingale flew back to her tree.

- One day the wind-up bird broke down.

- The Emperor had it fixed but it wasn't the same.

- The Emperor took ill and wanted the real bird.

- The maid fetched her and the Emperor got well.

- After that the bird came back every month.

- She sang about all the events of the kingdom.

TELL IT AGAIN!

Story Sources

ABOUT RETELLINGS, VARIATIONS, ADAPTATIONS,
AND NEW STORIES

The multicultural stories in this book are retold, varied, or adapted for young children. Some of the stories are told as new stories, which are structured and based on familiar tales. Many of the sources for the stories are anthologies and collections, noted in the following list. Additional references cited in the anthologies and collections are included. We have told some of these stories to children and remember many from our own childhoods.

Any retelling is the storyteller's remembrance of a story heard or read in the past. For example, "The Knee-High Man" is a retelling of a story we heard when we were children and later read in a collection of tales from the South. Our retelling stays true to the characters and the scenes.

A variation of a story is the storyteller's own flavoring with dialogue and inter-actions, which make the story come alive but remain true to the usual char-acters and the story actions. For example, "The Four Musicians" has phrases and interaction patterns that are spoken, with recurring phrases and repeated actions to make the story easy to tell. The storyteller may repeat the phrase multiple times for emphasis or state it once for dramatic effect.

Adaptations are more significant changes to the content of the story than sim-ple variations in dialogue or narration. An adaptation of a story may include adding or deleting characters or scenes to make it more interesting to an audi-ence or the readers. For example, in "The Great Game in the Sky" we added characters that are compatible with the theme and the other animals in the story.

A new story may be written based on the structure of an old story. For exam-ple, "Big City Mouse and Small Town Mouse" is a new story comparing life in both places, just as the Aesop fable of "City Mouse and Country Mouse" did. However, the scenes, settings, dialogue, and climax of the story differ. Both stories feature mice, and both stories compare the hazards and delights of life in both locations.

"Teeny, Tiny" is a familiar story in early childhood education circles. Folklorists call it an English tale; however, there are versions in other European collections. Versions of the tale can be found in Edna Johnson, Evelyn R. Sickels, Frances Clarke Sayers, and Carolyn Horovitz, *Anthology of Children's Literature* (Boston, 1977). Another version is Jill Bennett, *Teeny Tiny*, illustrated by Tomie dePaola (New York, 1986). In some of the old versions, the teeny tiny woman is so hungry that she keeps the bone to make soup. In the newer versions, she finds the bone for her dog.

"The Knee-High Man" is an African-American tale; however, there are numerous tales throughout the world about people seeking to become bigger, stronger, or richer, rather than appreciating who they are. "The Knee-High Man" was published by Julius Lester in *The Knee-High Man and Other Tales* (New York, 1972). We have also read the tale in Edna Johnson, Evelyn R. Sickels, Frances Clarke Sayers, and Carolyn Horowitz, *Anthology of Children's Literature* (Boston, 1977), and in Roger Abraham, *Afro-American Folktales: Stories from Black Traditions in the New World* (New York, 1995). The tale has also been told as "How the Knee-High Man Tried to Become Sizeable." We have heard Appalachian variations of the "Knee-High Man" told as a Jack tale.

"The Story of the Ugly Duckling" was originally published in a collection of *Fairy Tales from Hans Christian Andersen* (Denmark). These classic stories were written in Danish and later translated into English.

"Three Billy-Goats Gruff" is a Norwegian folktale, but it has been translated into so many languages that it is familiar in cultures throughout the world. The version presented here is our own. A popular children's picture book of the story is *The Three Billy-Goats Gruff* by Ellen Appleby (New York, 1984). We also read the story in numerous collections, including Edna Johnson, Evelyn R. Sickels, Frances Clarke Sayers, and Carolyn Horovitz, *Anthology of Children's Literature* (Boston, 1977). The earliest version found was Peter Christen Asbjornsen, *Popular Tales from the Norse*, translated by G. W. Dasent (New York, 1908).

"The Turtle and the Rabbit" is an adaptation of a famous Aesop fable, "The Tortoise and the Hare." As with other fables of the Aesop collection, a very important lesson is clearly illustrated in the events of the story. Several versions can also be found in *A Treasury of Bedtime Stories* (New York, 1981).

"Nail Soup" is a Czechoslovakian folktale. There are numerous versions, including the popular *Stone Soup*, which has soldiers rather than a tramp as the main characters and townspeople instead of an old woman.

"Johnny-Cake" is an English folktale; however, there are stories of runaway pancakes from Norway, runaway gingerbread men from the United States, runaway buns from Russia, and runaway rice cakes from Japan. Appalachian storytellers tell a variation of this tale, as well.

"The Flying Contest" is a folktale from Surinam. The tale contains "the clever one," a main character very much in the oral language, storytelling tradition. In addition, this short tale has another feature often heard in the told tale, a contest to settle an argument, to decide who is best, or to determine who should rule. We have read the version in Roger D. Abrahams' *Afro-American Folktales: Stories from Black Traditions in the New World* (New York, 1985).

"The Great Game in the Sky" is a variation of "The Great Lacrosse Game," a story from the Menominee people. Michael J. Caduto and Joseph Bruchac collected Native American stories and wrote of the significance of the tales in their book, *Keepers of the Night: Native American Stories and Nocturnal Activities for Children* (Golden, CO, 1994).

"Big City Mouse, Small Town Mouse" was inspired by Aesop's fable, "City Mouse, Country Mouse," a well-known tale that contrasts life in the city and the country. Our version tells a story that contrasts the big city and a small town, with a surprise twist at the end.

"Could Be Worse!" is a variation of a Yiddish folktale that has been told for hundreds of years and illustrates the age-old truth that no matter how bad things are they can always get worse. *Could Be Worse!* by James Stevenson is reprinted with permission of Greenwillow Books, a division of William Morrow and Company, Inc.

"Monkey's and Rabbit's Bad Habits" is a West African tale. Another version, by Jan M. Van Schuyver, appears in *Storytelling Made Easy with Puppets* (Phoenix, 1993). Schuyver sites two additional versions of the story: Frances Carpenter, *African Wonder Tales*, "Who Can Break a Bad Habit?" (New York, 1963) and Margaret Read MacDonald, *Twenty Tellable Tales*, "How to Break a Bad Habit" (New York, 1986).

"The Woman Who Wanted More Noise" is roughly based on *The Little Woman Wanted Noise* (1943, 1967). This book provides a wonderful story for telling. The variation in this book appears with permission from Checkerboard Press.

"The Lost Mitten With Tiny, Shiny Beads" is a retold version of "The Mitten," a Ukrainian folktale. Numerous storytellers and writers have retold this tale. Two of the most popular published versions were retold by Alvin Tresselt and by Jan Brett. As storytellers, we invite you to make the story your own by adding details or changing the animals. Invariably, a told story takes different forms with different tellers.

"The Four Musicians" is retold from a Grimm Fairy Tale. It was first published in 1819 in a collection of the brothers Grimm. The original name of the musicians in the story was Bremen, a town in Germany. This storyline has been told and retold in many different versions, including an Appalachian version by storyteller Don Davis.

"The Sparrow Who Couldn't Sing" is an adaptation of a picture book by Tony Maddox, *Spike the Sparrow Who Couldn't Sing* (London, 1989). In his book, Tony Maddox created a warm and humorous story that works well with young children. This story has been expanded and embellished for this collection to become a wonderful story for telling. The version of the story in this book appears with permission from Piccadilly Press Ltd.

"The King's Drum" is based on an Ashanti folktale. One version is included in Harold Dourlander, *The King's Drum and Other African Stories* (New York, 1962). *The King's Drum*, and many other stories from this region, are based on the spider trickster of the Ashanti people of Ghana. Anansi, half man and half spider, is also included in the folklore of Jamaica. Some of the Anansi stories have morals to teach but some tell how he tricks other animals in the forest. Anansi is admired because he is so clever and is thought to be the owner of all tales that are told.

"The Nightingale" is one of the Hans Christian Andersen tales. The story has been around since the 1800s and has been adapted and translated many times. Our version has been retold from several versions we read, and then shortened by our repeated tellings of the story to young children.

Storytelling References and Resources

Teeny, Tiny

Bennett, Jill. *Teeny Tiny*. Illustrated by Tomie dePaola. New York: Putnam, 1986.

Galdone, Paul. *The Teeny Tiny Woman*. New York: Houghton Mifflin, 1984.

Johnson, Edna, Evelyn R. Sickels, Frances Clarke Sayers, and Carolyn Horovitz. "Teeny-Tiny." *Anthology of Children's Literature*. 5th ed. Boston: Houghton Mifflin, 1977. (Johnson et. al. reference Jacobs, Joseph. *English Fairy Tales*. New York: Putnam, 1892.)

Robins, Arthur. *The Teeny Tiny Woman*. London: Candlewick Press, 1998.

Ziefert, Harriet. *Teeny Tiny Woman*. New York: Puffin, 1995.

The Knee-High Man

Abrahams, Roger D. "The Knee-High Man Gets Sizable." *Afro-American Folktales: Stories from Black Traditions in the New World*. New York: Pantheon Books, 1985. Abrahms references Carmer, Carl. *Stars Fell on Alabama*. New York: Doubleday, 1934.

Johnson, Edna, Evelyn R. Sickels, Frances Clarke Sayers, and Carolyn Horovitz. "The Knee-High Man." *Anthology of Children's Literature*. 5th ed. Boston: Houghton Mifflin, 1977. (Johnson et. al. reference Lester, Julius. *The Knee-High Man and Other Tales*. New York: Dial, 1972.)

Lester, Julius. *The Knee-high Man and Other Tales*. New York: Dutton, 1992.

Miller, William. *The Knee-High Man*. Layton, UT: Gibbs Smith, 1996.

The Story of the Ugly Duckling

Andersen's Fairy Tales. Illustrated by Troy Howell. Children's Classics Division of Dilithium Press, Avenel, NJ: 1988. Originally published as *Fairy Tales from Hans Christian Andersen*.

Brown, Margaret Wise. *The Ugly Duckling*. New York: Disney Press, 1994.

Mitchell, Adrian. *The Ugly Duckling*. New York: DK Publishing, 1994.

Sylvester, Charles. *Journeys Through Bookland*, Vol 1. Chicago: Belows-Reeve Co., 1922, 1932.

Three Billy Goats Gruff

Appleby, Ellen. *The Three Billy-Goats Gruff*. New York: Scholastic, 1984.

Carpenter, Stephen. *Three Billy Goats Gruff*. New York: HarperCollins, 1998.

Galdone, Paul. *Three Billy Goats Gruff*. New York: Houghton Mifflin, 1998.

Johnson, Edna, Evelyn R. Sickels, Frances Clarke Sayers, and Carolyn Horovitz. *Anthology of Children's Literature*. 5th ed. Boston: Houghton Mifflin, 1977. (Johnson et. al. reference Asbjornsen, Peter Christen. *Popular Tales from the Norse*. Translation by G. W. Dasent. New York: Putnam, 1908.)

The Turtle and the Rabbit

Dijs, Carla. *Tortoise and the Hare*. New York: Simon and Schuster, 1997.

Jones, Vernon (translation). *Aesop's Fables*. New York: Franklin Watts, 1912,1967,1969.

Power, Effie. "Fables" by Aesop. *Bag O' Tales*. New York: Dutton, 1934.

Sylvester, Charles. *Journeys Through Bookland*. Chicago: Bellows-Reeve, 1922,1932.

Wilson, Barbara Ker. *Animal Folk Tales*. New York: Grosset and Dunlap, 1968,1971.

Nail Soup

Brown, Marcia. *Stone Soup*. New York: Scribner, 1947.

McGovern, Ann. *Stone Soup*. Illustrated by Winslow P. Pels. New York: Scholastic, 1986.

Offen, Hilda. "Nail Soup." *A Treasury of Bedtime Stories*. New York: Simon and Schuster Books for Young Readers, 1981.

Ross, Tony. *Stone Soup*. New York: Dutton, 1992.

Johnny-Cake

Aylesworth, Jim. *The Gingerbread Man*. New York: Scholastic, 1998.

Baumgartner, Barbara. *The Gingerbread Man*. New York: DK Publishing, 1998.

Griffith, John W. and Charles H. Frey, eds. "Johnny Cake." *Classics of Children's Literature*. New York: Macmillan, 1981.

The Flying Contest or How Kunibre Became King of the Birds

Abrahams, Roger D. "The Flying Contest." In *Afro-American Folktales: Stories from Black Traditions in the New World*. Selected and edited by Roger D. Abrahams. New York: Pantheon Books, 1985. Abrahams references Herskovits, Melville J. and Frances S. *Suriname Folk-lore*. New York: Columbia University Press, 1936.

The Great Game in the Sky

Caduto, Michael J. and Joseph Bruchac. "The Great LaCrosse Game." *Keepers of the Night: Native American Stories and Nocturnal Activities for Children*. Golden, CO: Fulcrum Publishing, 1994.

Big City Mouse, Small Town Mouse

Brett, Jan. *Town Mouse, Country Mouse*. New York: Putnam, 1994.

Wallner, John. *City Mouse-Country Mouse and Two More Tales from Aesop*. New York: Scholastic, 1987.

"Could Be Worse!"

Zemach, Margot. *It Could Always Be Worse*. New York: Farrar Straus Giroux, 1976.

Monkey's and Rabbit's Bad Habits

MacDonald, Margaret R., ed. "How to Break a Bad Habit." *Twenty Tellable Tales*. Bronx, NY: Wilson, 1986.

VanSchuyver, Jan M. *Storytelling Made Easy with Puppets*. Phoenix, AZ: The Oryx Press, 1993. VanSchuyver cites two other versions of the story found in Carpentar, Frances. "Who Can Break a Bad Habit." *African Wonder Tales*. Illustrated by Joseph Escourido. New York: Doubleday, 1963.

The Woman Who Wanted More Noise

Teal, Val. *The Little Woman Wanted Noise*. New Edition. Skokie, Ill: Rand McNally, 1943.

The Lost Mitten with Tiny, Shiny Beads

Brett, Jan. *The Mitten: A Ukrainian Folktale*. New York: Putnam, 1990.

Koopmans, Loek. *Any Room for Me?* Edinburgh, Scotland: Floris Books.

Tresselt, Alvin. *The Mitten*. New York: Scholastic, 1964.

The Four Musicians

Grimm, Jacob, and Wilhelm K. Grimm. *Grimms' Tales for Young and Old: The Complete Stories*. Translated by Ralph Manheim. Garden City, NY: Doubleday, 1983.

Haviland, Virginia (retold from the brothers Grimm). *Favorite Fairy Tales Told in Germany*. Boston: Little, Brown and Company, 1959.

Kinscella, Hazel Gertrude. *Folk Tales from Many Lands*. Lincoln, NY: The University Publishing Company, 1939.

The Sparrow Who Couldn't Sing

Maddox, Tony. *Spike the Sparrow Who Couldn't Sing*. First Published in London, England: Piccadilly Press Limited, 1989. First Edition for the United States, 250 Wireless Boulevard, Hauppauge, NY 11788: Barron's Educational Series, 1989.

The King's Drum

Arneach, Lloyd. *The Animals' Ballgame*. Danbury, CT: Children's Press, 1995.

Courlander, Harold. *The King's Drum and Other African Stories*. New York: Harcourt, Brace and World, 1962.

The Nightingale

Anderson, Hans Christian. *The Nightingale*. New York: Simon and Schuster, 1991.

Griffith, John W. and Charles H. Frey, eds. "The Nightingale." *Classics of Children's Literature*. New York: Macmillan, 1981.

Offen, Hilda. *A Treasury of Bedtime Stories*. New York: Simon and Schuster Books for Young Readers, 1981.

TELL IT AGAIN!

Index

TELL IT AGAIN!

TELL IT AGAIN!